# JIBREEL

BY SULTAN-UL-WAIZEEN
MAULANA ABUL NOOR
MUHAMMAD BASHIR

TRANSLATED BY
SHAHID HUSSAIN

A unique collection of eighteen stories
relating to Sayyiduna Jibreel and his relationship
with the Messenger of Allah,
Peace and Blessings of Allah be upon him

Copyright © 2019

All rights reserved.

No part of this publication may be reproduced, stored in a retrieval system or transmitted in any form or by any means, electronic, mechanical, photocopying, recording or otherwise, without the written permission of the publishers.

ISBN 978-0-9571096-0-5

Second Edition, 2019

First Edition Printed in 2012

## Abul Noor Publications

Leicester, UK

publications@abulnoor.com

**Abul Noor**
PUBLICATIONS

## OUTSTANDING

Design, printed & bound in the UK by OUTSTANDING

Cover calligraphy *'Jibreel'* by OUTSTANDING

*'Durud Taaj'* Calligraphy by Hamid Iqbal Khan

بسم الله الرحمن الرحيم

In the name of Allah, most Merciful, most Kind

*'Say (O Prophet), 'Anyone who is an enemy of Jibreel he was the one who brought it down upon your heart, by the authority of Allah, confirming what came before it, as guidance and good news for the believers. Anyone who is an enemy of Allah and His angels and His Messengers and Jibreel and Mikaeel, then verily Allah is an enemy of the rejecters.'*

*(2:97-98)*

# Contents

Introduction ............................................. 9

Durud Taaj ............................................. 13

Why was Jibreel عليه السلام created? ......................... 17

1 | Jibreel's عليه السلام age ................................. 19
   Allah's First Creation
   Rays of *Noor*
   *Bashariyat* (humanness) of the Prophet ﷺ
   Temporary humanness
   The Prophet's ﷺ eating and drinking
   Maulana Rumi's Observation
   The Wahhabi's Jewish-like misdemeanours
   The Prophet ﷺ accepts a person's Islam on the condition
      of praying only two daily prayers
   The Prophet's ﷺ grave

2 | Khaleel & Jibreel عليهما السلام ......................... 35

3 | The dust of Jibreel's عليه السلام horse ................... 39

The weeping date trunk
The Prophet's ﷺ authority
The tree's intellect
Life in stones

**4 | Jibreel's ﷺ enquiry** ............................. 47

**5 | Jibreel's ﷺ speed** ............................... 49
How far is the sun from the earth?
Clarification

**6 | Jibreel ﷺ & Mary** ............................... 55
*Noor* in human clothing
Real and figurative attributes
Revelation of the Qur'an took one of two forms

**7 | The Hadith of Jibreel ﷺ** ......................... 65
Islam
Iman
Ihsan
Knowledge of the Day of Judgement
The Prophet of Allah's ﷺ knowledge of the Day of Judgement

**8 | Jibreel ﷺ, the Prophet's ﷺ *Wazir* (Minister)** . . . . . . . 73

The Prophet of Allah ﷺ is *Hakim* (ruler)

The Prophet of Allah ﷺ is *Mukhtar* (independent)

The Prophet of Allah ﷺ made impure things Haram

**9 | Jibreel ﷺ, the Prophet's ﷺ soldier** . . . . . . . . . . . . . . . . 81

Jibreel's ﷺ horse

**10 | Jibreel ﷺ and the accursed Abu Jahl** . . . . . . . . . . . . . 85

Madinah is free from Polytheism

**11 | Jibreel ﷺ and the green silk suit** . . . . . . . . . . . . . . . . . 89

Jibreel ﷺ sends salutations to Aisha

Sura Noor

Clothes

*Muzakki* (Purifier)

Mother

Mother of the Believers

Sayyida Aisha- Hadith scholar and jurist

Food at Sayyida Aisha's

Offering Fatiha is not an innovation

Allah wishes the happiness of His Beloved

**12 | Sayyiduna Ali & Jibreel ﷺ** . . . . . . . . . . . . . . . . . . . . . . 99

**13** | **Jibreel ﷺ, Mikaeel and the camel**..................101
  Allah's friends by His leave are removers of difficulties
  An angel in human form

**14** | **Jibreel ﷺ and the**
  **martyrdom news of Imam Hussain**..............105
  Response to a question
  But you perceive not
  The high status and rank of *Shahadat*
  How the Prophet ﷺ helped Imam Hussain at Karbala
  The Prophet's ﷺ tears
  Contempt of Ahle Bayt

**15** | **Jibreel's ﷺ observation**.........................115
  Molvi Ismail's observation

**16** | **Jibreel's ﷺ request**.............................119
  Waseela

**17** | **Jibreel ﷺ and the angel of death**................123

**18** | **Jibreel's ﷺ glad tidings**........................127

# Introduction

I am truly honoured and thankful for being given the opportunity to introduce the English rendition of *Jibreel Stories*, written by Sultanul Wa'izeen Maulana Abul Noor Muhammad Bashir and translated by Shahid Hussain.

Stories and narrations relating to the Archangel Jibreel ﷺ are of paramount importance to Muslims for several reasons. Firstly, because he was the prime deliverer of *Wahy* (Divine Revelation) to the Beloved Prophet ﷺ, we can begin to better appreciate the relationship between Allah and His Prophet ﷺ. Secondly, Jibreel's ﷺ role and service was not limited to our Prophet ﷺ alone; he met and served previous prophets and messengers too. It was Jibreel ﷺ who blew the spirit (*Ruh*) into Mary (peace be upon her) which subsequently led to the miraculous birth of Jesus ﷺ. It was Jibreel ﷺ who saved the sacrifice of Ibrahim's son ﷺ and replaced Ismail ﷺ with a sheep. Therefore, studying his life means we are given a more in-depth insight into Islam prior to the physical appearance of our Prophet ﷺ. Thirdly, Jibreel عليه السلام *per se* is a great and revered character in Islam, mentioned on several occasions in the Holy Qur'an. In fact, such is his rank amongst the angels that Allah has mentioned the angels in general and then coupled it with the mention of Jibreel عليه السلام separately. The Night of Power (Lailat al-Qadr), for instance, is described as the night when 'the angels descend and the *Ruh* (Jibreel عليه السلام) by Allah's permission with all decrees.' This literary style employed by Allah highlights the fact that though he is undoubtedly an angel, his rank and status warrants a separate mentioning by name.

Imam Abu Abdullah Muhammad bin Ahmad al-Ansari al-Qurtubi (d. 671 A.H.), a prominent commentator of the Holy Qur'an, defines the different pronunciations of the actual name *Jibreel* عليه السلام in his exegesis. He writes that there are ten different variations (i) Jibrīl; this variation is favoured by the people of Hijaz (ii) Jabrīl; this is the opinion of Hasan and Ibn Kathir (iii) Jabra'īl; as favoured by the people of Kufa (iv) Jabra'il (v) Jabra'ill (vi) Jabrā'il; as stated by Ikrama (vii) Jabrā'īl (viii) Jabra'yīl (ix) Jabra'īn (x) Jibrīn; this is the variation offered by Banu Asad.

Imam al-Qurtubi adds that the linguists differ as to whether Jibreel عليه السلام is actually an Arabic word or not.

Similarly, there is a dispute as to whether the name is a compound of two parts; *Jibr* and *Eel*. Many believe that *Jibr* means 'servant' and *Eel* refers to Allah, and collectively the name translates as 'the servant of Allah.'

In the famous and oft-recited 'Durud Taaj', Jibreel ﷺ is described as the 'servant of the Beloved Messenger' ('*Wa Jibreelu Khaadimuhu*'). Rather than an eloquent exaggeration with little basis, this statement is an established fact with sound evidence to support its authenticity. In a Hadith, we are informed that the Prophet ﷺ once removed his sandals. The Companions observed the Prophet's ﷺ actions and they too removed their footwear. Upon seeing this, the Prophet ﷺ asked them why they removed their footwear, since he had not told them to do so. Humbly, the Companions replied that they were merely following his actions. The Prophet ﷺ replied: 'I removed my sandals because Jibreel ﷺ just came to me and informed me that there is something harmful in them.'

Two things are deduced from this beautiful narration. Firstly, we learn the true extent to which the Companions adhered to the actions of the Beloved Messenger ﷺ. Even when the Prophet ﷺ performed a small act like removing his sandals, the Companions were eager to follow his Sunnah and example. Secondly, the role of Jibreel ﷺ, in relation to the Prophet ﷺ, was not simply to bring revelation to him from Allah. Rather, his role was to comprehensively and extensively serve the Beloved Messenger ﷺ. This meant that even when the sandals of the Prophet ﷺ contained something harmful and uncomfortable; it was part of the role and job description of Jibreel ﷺ to alleviate such unease from him.

I have no doubt that readers will appreciate the importance of this publication and that our Muslims, young and old, will benefit from these heart-warming and faith-strengthening stories of Jibreel ﷺ. May Allah make this work a means of forgiveness and mercy for the author and translator, Ameen.

**Hafiz Muhammad Ather Shahbaz Hussain al-Azhari**
Muharram 1433 Hijri /December 2011

© Hamid Iqbal Khan

# Durud Taaj

O Allah!
Send blessings and peace
Upon our Master and Patron Muhammad,
The Owner of the Crown and the Ascent
And the Buraq and the Standard,
The Repeller of affliction
And disease and drought and illness and pain,
His name is written on High served
And graved in the Tablet and Pen,
The Leader of all Arabs and non Arabs,
Whose body is sanctified, fragrant
And pure illuminated in the House and Sanctuary,
The Sun of brightness,
The full Moon in darkness,
The Foremost One in the Highest fields,
The Light of Guidance,
The Cave of refuge for mortals,
The Light that dispels the Night,
The Best-Natured One, the Intercessor of Nations,
Allah is His Protector,

# Jibreel is his Servant.

The Buraq is his Mount the Ascent is his Voyage,
Two bow lengths or nearer is his desire ,
His desire is his Goal, and he has found his goal.
The Master of the Messengers,
The Seal of the Prophets,
The Intercessor of Sinners,
The Friends of strangers,
The Mercy of the worlds,
The comfort of those that burn with love,
The goal of those who yearn,
The Sun of Knowers, the Lamp of Travellers,
The Light of those brought near,
the Friend of the poor
And destitute, the Master of Humans and Jinns,
The Prophet of the Two Sanctuaries, the Imam of the
Two Qiblas, Our means in the two worlds,
The Owner of *Qaba Qausain*,
The Beloved of the Lord of the Two Easts
and Two Wests,
The Grandfather of Al Hasan and Al Hussain,
Our Patron and the Patron of Humans and Jinns,
Abul Qasim Muhammad son of Abdullah,

A Light from the Light of Allah
O you who yearn for the light of His Beauty Send
Blessings and utmost Greetings of Peace upon him
and his family.

# Why was Jibreel عليه السلام created?

Sidi Abdul Aziz Ad-Dabbagh, may Allah be pleased with him, in *Al-Ibreez Sharif* writes:

*'Wa Sayiduna Jibreel alayhis salaam innama khuliqa le khidamattun nabi sallal laahu alaihi wasallam'*

'Sayyiduna Jibreel عليه السلام was created in order to serve the Prophet of Allah ﷺ'

The Poet Hassan Mian expresses this fact in the following way:

*Khuda neh jab Azal mein nehmateh taqseem farma'ee*
*Likhee Jibreel ki taqdeer mein khidmat Rasool ki*

In the beginning when Allah distributed
His divine favours and blessings
He wrote in Jibreel's عليه السلام favour
the service of Muhammad ﷺ

Ad-Dabbagh states further that if Jibreel ﷺ was to have lived for hundreds and thousands of years before he was created, he would not have attained even a fourth of the knowledge that the Messenger of Allah ﷺ has. Furthermore, the honour and status Jibreel ﷺ has is due to the company (*Suhba*) of the Prophet of Allah ﷺ.

# Jibreel's عليه السلام age

The Prophet of Allah ﷺ once asked Jibreel عليه السلام about his age. Jibreel عليه السلام replied: "O Prophet! I don't know my exact age but I can tell you that there is a star in the fourth heaven which appears after every seventy thousand years. I have seen that star shine seventy thousand times." The Prophet of Allah ﷺ said: "I swear by the honour of my Lord, I am that star."

*(Ruhul Bayan)*

Allah says in the opening verse of the Holy Qur'an 'All perfections are for Allah, Lord of the worlds.' And when He praises His Messenger He says "We have not sent you but as a mercy to all the worlds." Allah is Lord of the worlds and Muhammad is the mercy to all the worlds. In Arabic *Alameen* is the plural of *Alam* – world. For every world that exists, Allah is its Lord, Creator, Sustainer and for every world that exists Prophet Muhammad ﷺ has been sent as a mercy towards it. The Prophet's ﷺ mercy extends to all of creation from the beginning of time because ever since the beginning of creation there has been a world and there cannot be for one moment where there exists a world and the Prophet of Allah ﷺ was not sent as a mercy for it.

The meaning of the word *Rabb* is to cherish, sustain. Allah the Almighty has used this word in the Qur'an for Himself but he has also described parents as *Rabb*.

> 'O my Lord! Have mercy on both of them
> as they brought me up (*Rabbayaani*) when I was an infant.'
> *(17:24)*

Allah describes parents as *Rabb* because parents have love and care for their children. If such qualities did not exist then Allah would have never called them *Rabb*. The affection, love and care in parents are a sign of their mercy towards their children. Hence to be a *Rabb*, mercy is also needed. Before Allah made known His Mastery of all the worlds, He created the mercy for all the worlds. If the mercy to all the worlds was not created then the Lord of all the worlds would not have been known and would have remained hidden. A Hadith Qudsi recorded by Shaykh Ahmad Sirhindi (may Allah be pleased with him) in his well known *Maktubaat* says: "O beloved! If you did not exist I would not have revealed My Lordship." This Hadith Qudsi shows that Allah made his Lordship known by creating the Mercy to all the worlds first.

# Allah's first creation

Abd al-Razzaq has reported with his chain of transmission from Jabir ibn Abdullah al-Ansari ﷺ that: "I asked: Ya Rasoolallah! May my father and mother be sacrificed for you! Tell me of that which Allah created before anything else? He said: "O Jabir verily Allah created the light (*Noor*) of your Prophet Muhammad ﷺ from His *Noor*, before He created anything else. And this *Noor*, (of your prophet), remained by the power of Allah as long as Allah willed and at that time there was neither the tablet (*Lawh*), nor the pen (*Qalam*), no paradise (*Jannah*), no hell (*Naar*), and neither any angel. None of the heavens and nor the earth, neither the sun, nor the moon, nor human or jinn existed. When Allah wished to create something else, He made four parts of that *Noor*. From the first part He created the pen (*Qalam*); from the second the tablet (*Lawh*); from the third the throne (*Arsh*) and He divided the fourth part into four more. From the first of this fourth part He created the bearers of the throne (*Arsh*); from the second He created the footstool (*Kursi*); from the third the rest of the angels and He divided the fourth part into four more; from the first He created the heavens; from the second He created the earth; from the third He created paradise and hell; and He divided the fourth part into four more; from the first he created the light of the believer's (*mu'min*) eyes; from the second part the light in their hearts; from the third part the light of solace and that is the *Kalima: La ilaha Illallah Muhammadur Rasoolallah*."

We learn from this extraordinary account that the first creation was the *Noor-e-Muhammadi* and this had to be because he is *Rahmatul lil alameen*, Mercy of all the worlds. By the act of creation Allah's *Rabubiyyat*, (the quality of being the sustainer, cherisher and preserver) became known and for this to be known, *Rahmat* had to exist. In other words, *Rahmat* had to be in existence for Allah's Lordship to be known. The beginning of creation had to begin with the *Noor* of the Prophet of Allah ﷺ otherwise there would have been a moment when a world existed without him being sent as a mercy to it. As Allah says in the Qur'an that "And we have sent you not but as a Mercy to all the worlds" therefore it is imperative that the Prophet of Allah ﷺ was created first. It is Allah's will that the *Noor* of this Mercy to all the worlds was created first and then the rest of creation was made thereafter. Jibreel ؑ is also part of Allah's creation. His creation was after that of the Messenger of Allah ﷺ despite the fact that the angels were created long before Adam ؑ was. Despite living for millions of years as the Hadith illustrates, Jibreel ؑ came after the *Noor* of Sayyiduna Muhammad Mustafa ﷺ.

# Rays of *Noor*

In the commentary of *Sahih al-Bukhari*, Imam Qastalani, may Allah be pleased with him, in narrating the *Noor* Hadith says that when Allah created the *Noor-e-Muhammadi* ﷺ, time did not exist, nor did the *Lawh* or *Qalam* the *Arsh* or *Kursi* nor *Jannat* or *Jahannam*. There was absolutely nothing but Allah and the *Noor-e-Muhammadi*. When Allah intended to create the rest of creation He divided the *Noor-e-Muhammadi* into four parts:

- From the first part He created the pen (*Qalam*)
- From the second part He created the preserved tablet (*Lawh Mahfooz*)
- From the third part He created the throne (*Arsh*)
- From the fourth part He divided into four further parts

- The first portion He created the Bearers of the *Arsh* (Throne)
- The second portion He created the Kursi
- The third portion He created all the angels
- The fourth portion He divided into four further parts

- The first part He created the heavens
- The second part He created the earth
- The third part He created the Jannat and Jahannam
- The fourth part He divided into four further parts

- The first part He created the *Noor* of the eyes of the Believers
- The second part He created the light of *Marifat* (gnosis) in their hearts
- The third part He created the rest of creation.

*(Al-Mawahib al-Laduniyya)*

We learn from this that the *Noor-e-Muhammadi* ﷺ has precedence over all creation because all creation is a result of his Noor. Imam Qastalani's narration illustrates clearly that all of creation has come into being because of *Noor-e-Muhammadi* ﷺ.

## *Bashariyat* (human nature) of the Prophet ﷺ

The Prophet of Allah ﷺ was created before Jibreel علیہ السلام and he was created before Adam علیہ السلام and we know that our Prophet ﷺ was in existence before Adam علیہ السلام was created. The Prophet of Allah ﷺ was Prophet before man was made as the following Hadith testifies. "I was Prophet when Adam علیہ السلام was still between water and clay." The *Noor-e-Muhammadi* shone well before Adam علیہ السلام was created. If *Bashariyat* (humanness) were a requirement of Prophethood, then this process would have started with Adam علیہ السلام. But as the Prophet of Allah ﷺ said: "I was Prophet when Adam علیہ السلام was still between soil and water." *Bashariyat* is not a condition but for our guidance, it is necessary for prophets to come in the garb of humanness. Hence the reality of the Prophet of Allah ﷺ is *Noor*, but we know him and recognise him in his human form. Prophethood then is not dependent on *Bashariyat* but for the sake and guidance of mankind, Allah made it a requirement.

## Temporary humanness

Imam Waasti, may Allah be pleased with him, in his commentary of the verse "...The hand of Allah is over their hands..." (48:10) says that Allah gives us the news that His Prophet's ﷺ humanness is temporary and not permanent. He like most other scholars of Ahle Sunna wal Jama'a is of the belief that the Prophet's ﷺ humanness is temporary and not real.

## The Prophet's ﷺ eating & drinking

The people who say that the Prophet of Allah ﷺ is only human point out that he too like us ate and drank. Hence there is no difference between him and us. Without doubt the Messenger of Allah ﷺ ate and drank, but his eating and drinking was of a different nature. First of all, the Prophet of Allah ﷺ is not dependent on food as he said: "I am not like you. In the night my Lord feeds me with His sustenance" (*Bukhari*). When the Prophet of Allah ﷺ is provided by the Lord Almighty directly what need then for worldly food? So why did the Prophet ﷺ eat and drink? The simple reason for this was to establish a Sunnah so that his Ummah could eat and drink. By eating and drinking he told us what Halal is and what is Haram, what is liked and what is disliked. In the commentary of *Sahih al-Bukhari*, Imam Qastalani, may Allah be pleased with him, says: "The Prophet of Allah's ﷺ outward appearance is human but his inward (and natural) state is *Malakuti* (angelic). The human traits like eating, drinking, sleeping he adopted was not out of his personal need but it was solely for the benefit of his followers and believers so that they could live normally." In other words if he did not eat and drink then eating and drinking for his followers would have been forbidden. He ate not out of need but out of love and compassion for his Ummah so that they could live comfortably. If the Prophet of Allah ﷺ did not eat we would not know what was permissible and what was forbidden. The Prophet of Allah ﷺ came as *al-Mu'allim*, the teacher of Mankind.

# Maulana Rumi's observation

Maulana Rumi, may Allah be pleased with him, in his *Masnawi* says:

> **Whatever we eat eventually turns into waste**
> **But whatever he ate turned into Noor**

The Mother of the Believers Sayyida Aisha ﷺ says that she said to the Prophet of Allah ﷺ: "Ya Rasoolallah! When you go to relieve yourself there is no waste. Instead I find a beautiful smell." The Prophet of Allah ﷺ replied: "Don't you know that my body was created with the people of Paradise, whatever comes out, the earth consumes it." *(al-Khasa'is al-Kubra)*

In another narration the Prophet of Allah ﷺ said that the earth consumes the human waste of all prophets so that nobody can see it. We challenge people to bring even a fabricated Hadith saying that somebody has seen the waste of the Prophet ﷺ. The people who maintain that they are of the likeness of the Prophet ﷺ are dirty themselves.

# The Wahhabi's Jewish-like misdemeanours

*Tafsir Ruhul Bayan* is an exegesis of the Holy Qur'an in the Arabic language by Shaykh Allama Ismail Haqqi, may Allah be pleased with him. It is a commentary that is authenticated and is regarded as one of the most famous commentaries of the Holy Qur'an. Moreover the Tafsir is classical in the sense that it affirms the beliefs and doctrines of Ahle Sunnah wal Jama'a. On the orders of the Wahhabi regime, a scholar in Makkah by the name of Shaykh Muhammad Ali Saabooni Najdi removed all passages in *Ruhul Bayan* that authenticated the beliefs of Ahle Sunnah and was in direct contradiction to those purported by Muhammad bin Abdul Wahhab Najdi. Having 'edited' the Tafsir the volumes were re-launched in Saudi Arabia. A fellow scholar sent me a copy of the revised *Ruhul Bayan* from there. I examined the book and found that the Wahhabis had blatantly imitated the Jews by removing and tampering with the classical texts. They had removed the story of Jibreel ﷺ and the vision of the star because the story was in clear contradiction to the heretical Najdi beliefs. The story illustrates that the Prophet of Allah ﷺ is made of *Noor* and that he was the first of creation, something that Wahhabis can never accept. Furthermore the commentary on the verse of the Qur'an "The hand of Allah is over their hands..." was removed as it stated the words of Allama Ismail Haqqi that the Prophet of Allah's ﷺ humanness was temporary and not real. The Wahhabi's who have nothing but contempt for the Beloved of Allah ﷺ tampered the classical texts of Islam such as *Tafsir Ruhul Bayan* to suit their needs.

## The Prophet ﷺ accepts a person's Islam on the condition of praying only two daily prayers

In the *Musnad* of Imam Ahmad, may Allah be pleased with him, we find a Hadith in which a man came to the Prophet of Allah ﷺ and said that he was willing to embrace Islam but on the condition that he prayed two of the daily prayers and not the obligatory five. The Prophet of Allah ﷺ accepted it and made him read the *Kalima*.

This Hadith clearly demonstrates the authority which Allah Almighty has given to the Prophet ﷺ. Everyone knows that Islam requires praying five times a day; a fact established from the Qur'an and Sunnah but here the Messenger of Allah ﷺ exercised his authority in accepting the Islam of a person who would only pray twice a day. The same person a while later told the Prophet of Allah ﷺ that he would now pray five times a day.

Muhaddith Aazam Maulana Muhammad Sardar Ahmad of

Faisalabad wrote to me saying that he purchased the *Musnad* of Imam Ahmad and read it from cover to cover but could not find the Hadith about the acceptance of Islam on two daily prayers. He wrote to me asking for the reference page of the Hadith from my copy, which I duly gave to him. He again looked at his copy and did not find the narration. The reason why he could not find it was because the Wahhabis published the copy he purchased. They had reprinted the *Musnad* of Imam Ahmad and removed this Hadith because it illustrated the authority of the Prophet of Allah ﷺ. The Wahhabis of the Indian Subcontinent spent thousands of rupees just to remove this narration. Similarly a Wahhabi sponsored bookstore in Karachi reprinted *Gunya al-Talibeen*. In it they removed the Hadith saying that Taraweeh prayer in Ramadan is twenty rakats and heavily emphasised the Hadith saying that it was eight rakats instead. There are countless more examples of tampering of the classical texts of Islam by the Wahhabis.

## The Prophet's ﷺ grave

When the Ottomans had control over the Holy Hijaz region, they took due care and attention to honouring the Holy Sites. At the face of the Prophet's ﷺ grave the Ottoman's had scribed the following verse:

'And if when they do injustice upon their souls,
then O beloved, they should come to you and then beg
forgiveness from Allah and the Messenger of Allah should
intercede for them, then surely, they would find Allah
most Relenting, Merciful.'

*(4:64)*

This beautiful verse of the Holy Qur'an instructs sinful Muslims to go to the Prophet of Allah ﷺ and seek Allah's forgiveness in his presence. Because this verse of the Qur'an explicitly implies the *Waseela* (mediation) and *Shafa'at* (intercession) of the Prophet ﷺ, the Wahhabis removed this verse from above the Prophet's ﷺ grave. They replaced that verse with the following:

'And Muhammad is not a father like you
but the seal of Prophets...'

*(33:40)*

In 1954 I went to perform the Hajj and the former verse was above the Prophet's ﷺ grave. But six years later it had gone and the latter verse was scribed instead. Tampering with the words of Allah in the Holy Qur'an like how the Jews did with the Torah is not possible because Allah has taken the responsibility of protecting it. Allah says in the Qur'an:

'Verily it is We who have revealed this discourse (i.e.

**Qur'an) and verily we are the guardian (of it).'**

*(15:9)*

Otherwise the Wahhabis given the chance would have removed the following verses of the Qur'an because their meaning and essence clash with their puritanical and distorted beliefs.

**'And we have sent you not but as a Mercy to all the worlds.'**

*(21:107)*

**'O Communicator of the Unseen (Nabi)! Truly we have sent you as a witness and a bearer of glad tidings and as a timely warner and an inviter to Allah by His command and as a brightening light.'**

*(33:45-46)*

**'Undoubtedly there has come to you a light (*Noor*) and a luminous book.'**

*(5:15)*

**'And if when they do injustice upon their souls, then O beloved, they should come to you and then beg forgiveness from Allah and the messenger of Allah should intercede for them, then surely, they would find Allah most relenting, merciful.'**

*(4:64)*

**'...The hand of Allah is over their hands...'**

*(48:10)*

'(And O My Beloved!) The dust that you did throw, it was not you who threw it at them when you threw, but Allah threw in order to bestow a favour upon the believers...'
*(8:17)*

'...He (i.e. the Prophet of Allah) makes lawful to them clean
and pure things and prohibits them from
the unclean and impure...'
*(7:157)*

Ala Hazrat Imam Ahmed Raza Khan says:

> *Zaalimo! Mahboob ka haqq tha yehi*
> *Ishq ke badle adaawat kijiye*

O tyrants! Is this what the Beloved's rights are?
In return for his love, you give enmity?

• 2 •

# *Khaleel* and Jibreel ﷺ

When Ibrahim ﷺ was about to be catapulted into Nimrod's fire, Jibreel ﷺ went to him and told him to supplicate to Allah to save him. Ibrahim ﷺ however was not worried about his predicament. Jibreel ﷺ asked him why. He asked Jibreel ﷺ: "Who lit the fire?" Jibreel ﷺ replied: "Nimrod did." "And who put this idea in Nimrod's head?" asked Ibrahim. Jibreel ﷺ replied: "Allah did." Ibrahim ﷺ then said: *"ilmuhu bi-haaliy kafaaniy`an su'aaliy,* He has knowledge of my state; there is no need for me to say." It is the wish of Allah that I am tested in this way, therefore I do not require your services."

*(Nuzhatul Majaalis)*

The fire of Nimrod was a test of Ibrahim's devotion to Allah. Despite building a huge fire Nimrod could not even bring the slightest harm to Allah's prophet, Indeed Allah is the protector of those who remember and fear Him. Ibrahim ﷺ did not accept Jibreel's ﷺ offer because it would have taken him away from the real test Allah was giving him.

In *Nuzhatul Majaalis* it is also reported that when Ibrahim ﷺ was about to be placed in the catapult for the fire, the angels of the heavens and earth shuddered at the prospect of his fate. They called upon their Lord and said: "O Allah! Your *Khaleel* is about to enter Nimrod's fire whereas there is no one on the earth except him glorifying You and propagating Your Oneness. Give us permission to help." Allah replied to His angels: "He is indeed My *Khaleel*, other than him I have no other *Khaleel* and there is no other Lord for him except Me. If he does not seek help, then you do not get in between the affairs of Me and My *Khaleel*. Let Me know about it or my *Khaleel*." The angels of water appeared before Sayyiduna Ibrahim ﷺ and said: "If you wish we will extinguish the fire for you." The angels of the wind then appeared and said: "O Ibrahim ﷺ! We will extinguish the fire for you with your permission." He said to the angels of water and wind: "I have no need for you. My Lord is sufficient for me." It was after this that the leader of the angels, Jibreel ﷺ came and offered his assistance.

Sayyiduna Ibrahim's ﷺ contentment and acceptance of his fate for the trial he was being put through shows what perfect reliance he had in Allah Almighty. Ibrahim ﷺ had no other wish other than the wish and will of his Lord. This is why he rejected the assistance offered to him by the angels of the water and wind and above all, the help of Jibreel ﷺ. By not accepting this help, we should not think that to seek help from Allah's friends is *Shirk* (polytheism). If somebody thinks that then we ask them was it *Shirk* for the angels to ask Allah to help Sayyiduna Ibrahim ﷺ? Furthermore did the angels offer false hope to Ibrahim ﷺ in that critical situation if they really could not help him? Moreover did Allah scold the angels for making such a request in the first place? Wouldn't Allah have told his angels not to commit *Shirk* by helping someone or seeking help from other than Allah? We learn from this that the angels could have assisted him in this test, but he refused it because Allah was testing him. The fact of the matter is that Allah's friends (*Awliya*) and angels can help with the power of Allah. If he wanted to he could have called for help but Ibrahim ﷺ was being tested by Allah and refused the assistance. This was a trial from Allah to one of His dearest and greatest prophets. Prophet Ibrahim's ﷺ contentment and satisfaction in Allah's will was so complete that he passed the trial given to him.

• 3 •

# The dust of Jibreel's ﷺ horse

Amongst the Israelites was a goldsmith called Samiri, who came from the tribe of Samara. This tribe worshipped idols. When Samiri joined the Israelites and accepted their faith, he still had inclinations towards idols. This inclination was sparked again when they saw the cow-shaped idol at the Red Sea. So when Musa ﷺ went to Mount Toor (Sinai) to receive the revelations, Samiri found his opportunity to make an idol. Samiri used gold and jewellery to make a calf-shaped idol. He then put some soil on it giving it the ability to speak. The Israelites then began to worship it. Musa ﷺ came back furious to see that within the time he was away, the Israelites had committed idol worship. He asked Samiri what he had done. Samiri told Musa that at the time of the Red Sea miracle, he saw Jibreel ﷺ on a horse, which emitted green smoke as it went past. He went to where the horse went by and grabbed hold of some of the soil. He placed this special soil on the golden calf that enabled it to speak. He said to Musa ﷺ that he liked the

**idol and was proud of it. Musa ﷷ expelled him and told him that his punishment was that from now on whoever touched him they and him would be inflicted with a severe fever. Hence anybody that went near him would fall ill, as well as Samiri. He went around telling people not to come near him. He eventually went into exile in the jungle where he lived out the rest of his life in disgrace.**

*(Ruhul Bayan; in the commentary of 20:95-104)*

The status of Jibreel's ﷷ horse is that the ground it runs on is blessed with life. Such a horse was created for Jibreel's ﷷ use. And as we know Jibreel ﷷ is the servant of our Prophet ﷺ. So what can be said about the city and moreover the shrine in which the Prophet of Allah ﷺ is resting in? Can we imagine what will be the status and blessings of that soil in which Allah's prophets (peace upon them all) are buried? Samiri saw the benefits in Jibreel's ﷷ dust. So why is it that some so-called Muslims today say that Allah's prophets cannot do anything for us?

Imam Malik gave a fatwa that someone who had said that 'The soil of Madinah is bad' should be given thirty lashes and jailed. The man had some standing in the community but Imam Malik said: "His head should be cut off. He claims that the soil in which the Prophet of Allah ﷺ is resting is not good!"

## The weeping date trunk

When the Prophet's ﷺ Mosque was being built it did not have a pulpit from which the Prophet ﷺ could deliver his sermons. The Prophet of Allah ﷺ would rest against a dried date trunk and would deliver his sermons from there. The Noble Companions had an idea of constructing a pulpit for the Prophet ﷺ. They asked for permission, which he gave. Friday came and the Prophet ﷺ climbed the new pulpit to give the Friday sermon. It was when the Prophet of Allah ﷺ was delivering his sermon that he and the Noble Companions heard a sound like that of a crying baby camel (*Bukhari*). The Companions were stunned at the crying noises the date trunk was making. Sahl bin Saad ؓ, says that when the trunk began to cry, the people present also began to cry (*al-Khasa'is al-Kubra*). The Prophet of Allah ﷺ disembarked his new pulpit, went to the date trunk and embraced it. The Prophet of Mercy ﷺ then said: "Had I not comforted this trunk, it would have continued to cry like this till the Day of Judgement."

*(Hujjatullah alal Alameen)*

This miracle of the Prophet ﷺ is more amazing than that of his predecessor, Jesus son of Mary ؑ when he brought the dead back to life. Jesus son of Mary ؑ brought back to life beings that once had life inside them. Jesus ؑ by Allah's command would recapture that soul and replace it into that being, thus bringing the dead back to life. This was indeed a great miracle of the Messiah. But what the Final Messenger ﷺ did was to place life, feelings and emotions into those objects that did not have life in the first place. The dried-out date trunk had developed such intense feelings towards the Prophet of Mercy ﷺ during the time that the Prophet ﷺ delivered his sermons leaning against it. When the trunk realised the Prophet of Allah ﷺ was delivering his sermon from elsewhere, it started to cry in the pain of separation from that being that was sent as a Mercy for all creation.

## The Prophet's ﷺ authority

The Messenger of Allah ﷺ having consoled the date trunk said to it: "Be quiet. If you wish, I will replant you in Paradise where the pious and noble prophets and friends of Allah will eat your fruits. Or if you wish I can replant you and make you fruitful and green once again."

The date tree took the option of bliss in the hereafter and eternal company with the being it loved.

SubhanAllah! Look how great the status and honour is of

our Prophet ﷺ. He is talking to a dried date trunk and was giving it a choice between this world and the hereafter. The words of the narration are "I will" meaning that the Prophet of Allah ﷺ had the authority to grant whatever he was asked for. Allah has given the Prophet ﷺ such authority and power to give to the creation otherwise, the Prophet ﷺ would never utter things that were against his abilities. Now let us compare this fact with the statement of Molvi Ismail Dehlvi who says in *Taqwiyatul Iman*: "Whoever's name is Muhammad or Ali has authority over nothing." (Ma'azallah - Allah forbid) The date trunk is indeed most fortunate as it is a tree of Paradise as a result of acknowledging and accepting the Prophet's ﷺ authority. Should we not then firmly believe in what the Messenger of Allah has preached or believe the words of Molvi Ismail Dehlvi?

## The tree's intellect

**A Bedouin challenged the Prophet of Allah ﷺ to show him a miracle if he was who he claimed to be. The Prophet of Allah ﷺ told the man to go and call the tree over to him. The man did as he was told. The tree heard this command and lifted itself out of the ground dragging its roots with it and went to the Prophet of Allah ﷺ. The tree then offered**

its salaam. The man then asked the Prophet ﷺ to tell the tree to return to its place. The tree obediently followed the Prophet's ﷺ orders and went exactly back to its own place. The man on seeing this accepted Islam immediately and asked the Prophet ﷺ whether he could prostrate to him. He told him that that was not allowed but permitted him to kiss the hands and feet of Rasoolallah ﷺ.

*(Hujjatullah Alal Alameen)*

This is the blessing of the Prophet of Mercy, ﷺ that a tree had the sense of recognition and intellect and obeyed the command of the Prophet of Allah ﷺ. The Sufis commenting on this story say that when the tree heard that the Prophet ﷺ was calling it, it moved backwards, forwards and then side to side, in other words it was uprooting itself. The Sufis say that the tree came into *Wajd* (spiritual ecstasy) at the presence of the Prophet of Allah ﷺ.

## Life in stones

Anas ؓ says that the Messenger of Allah ﷺ picked up a few pebbles in his blessed hand. "They (i.e. the pebbles) began to do *Tasbih* and we could hear it."

*(al-Khasa'is al-Kubra)*

These stories clearly illustrate the effect the Prophet of Allah ﷺ had on creation. This is not surprising because the horse of the Prophet's ﷺ servant Jibreel ؑ had such qualities.

Ala Hazrat Imam Ahmad Raza Khan says in some beautiful words:

> *Chamak tuj se pa'the hein sub paaneh waleh,*
> *Mera dil be chamka deh chamka neh waleh*

'You sparkle everyone and everyone takes from you,
Sparkle my heart as well O one who sparkles!'

· 4 ·

# Jibreel's ﷺ enquiry

Jibreel ﷺ once sent the Pharaoh a letter asking him his opinion of what he thought should be the suitable punishment for a person who was loyal and who looked after wealth, but was ungrateful for it and a person that denied the need to be grateful to the extent that he believed that he was infallible? Pharaoh replied that such a person should be drowned. So when the Pharaoh was drowning in the Red Sea, Jibreel ﷺ came and showed him the ruling he had made.

*(Khazahinul Irfan)*

The four earthly elements: fire, water, soil and wind were made by Allah to serve and to be subservient to mankind. But when man transgresses and goes beyond the acceptable boundaries of behaviour and begins to be boastful and arrogant then these four elements can work to destroy such people. Water is an enormous favour of Allah. We use water to wash and bathe, to drink and cook and many other essential things. Yet if Allah wishes, water could destroy us just as it destroyed the Pharaoh.

# Jibreel's السلام speed

One day, the Messenger of Allah ﷺ asked Sayyiduna Jibreel السلام if he had ever travelled at his fastest speed. Jibreel السلام told the Prophet ﷺ that he had travelled at full speed on four occasions. The Prophet of Allah ﷺ then asked him when those four occasions were.

The first occasion Jibreel السلام recalled was when Ibrahim السلام was placed in Nimrod's fire. At the time he was near the *Arsh* (throne) when Allah ordered him to go and cool the fire of Nimrod so that he was not harmed. He left the *Arsh* and descended the seven heavens and reached earth in time to cool the fire. The second time was when Ibrahim السلام had placed his beloved son Ismail السلام on a stone in Mina and was about to sacrifice him for the sake of Allah. Allah ordered Sayyiduna Jibreel السلام to quickly go to the heavens and take a lamb, then rush to Mina and replace Ismail with the lamb before Ibrahim struck the knife. He did so before the time it took Ibrahim to raise his hand with the knife.

The third case was when the brothers of Yusuf ﷺ placed him in the well with a rope. As the brothers were about to throw him in, Allah ordered him to go to Canaan and save Yusuf ﷺ before he landed at the bottom of the well. He reached the well and placed his wings underneath Yusuf ﷺ, thus cushioning his fall.

The fourth time he travelled at full speed was when the Holy Prophet ﷺ had damaged one of his blessed teeth in battle. Allah ordered him to stop the blood reaching the ground. Otherwise, until the end of the world, no plant or tree would ever grow. So hearing this he dashed from the heavens and reached him and saved the blood with his wings.

*(Ruhul Bayan)*

How far is the earth from the sky? The Prophet of Allah ﷺ tells us "the distance between the earth and heavens is five hundred years." He then went on to explain that "between two heavens is the distance of the earth and the first sky" (*Mishkat Sharif*). So the distance between the earth and the sky is five hundred years travelling and the gap between the first heaven and the second heaven is five hundred years travelling. Above the seven heavens is *Sidra tul Muntahaa* –The Lote Tree. At *Sidra* we find the home of Jibreel ﷺ and on the night of Miraj it was here that he told the Prophet of Allah ﷺ that he could travel no further with him on this glorious journey because

*Sidra* was his limit. Jibreel ﷺ explained to the Prophet ﷺ that if he went any further his wings would melt and be destroyed. The Prophet of Allah ﷺ went alone from *Sidra* where he met Allah Almighty.

## How far is the sun from the earth?

The Sun is approximately 93 million miles away from earth. If the Sun is that far away, just imagine how far *Sidra tul Muntahaa* is from earth? Scientists have managed to calculate the speed of light, the speed at which light travels. Light years are used to measure the distance of stars, solar systems and galaxies. The speed of light is about 186,000 miles per second, which if converted into per hour is 669,600,000 (six hundred and sixty nine million six hundred thousand) miles per hour. Amazing! We can work out using a calculator that it takes approximately 8 minutes for the sun's light to travel 186,000 miles per second and cover the distance of 93 million miles from the sun to the earth. Can we begin to imagine the time it would take travelling at the speed of light to go from the earth to *Sidra*?

So what sort of time frame was Jibreel ﷺ working in when he had to go from the *Sidra* to earth? Prophet Ibrahim ﷺ was catapulted into Nimrod's fire when Allah ordered Jibreel ﷺ to go and cool the fire and to make it into a garden. The knife was inches from Ismail's ﷺ neck when Allah ordered Sayyiduna Jibreel ﷺ to go to Mina via the Heavens with a lamb and save Prophet Ismail ﷺ. Prophet Yusuf ﷺ was falling into the well when Jibreel ﷺ was ordered by Allah to go and save him from being hurt in one of the disused wells of Canaan. And the Prophet of Mercy ﷺ was hurt when Jibreel ﷺ rushed to wipe up the blood of the Prophet ﷺ before it touched the ground of Uhud.

We learn that Jibreel's ﷺ speed is much faster than that of the speed of light and as we learnt at the beginning of this book, Jibreel ﷺ was created by Allah to serve the Prophet of Allah ﷺ. If the servant's speed is so fast, can we comprehend the speed of the Master who is the *Noor* of Allah? If the speed of the servant is beyond imagination and is miraculous then surely the speed of the Master is beyond human intellect and comprehension. If we put this story into perspective then we can have firm belief in the miracle of the Night Journey and Ascension. We can accept the fact that the Prophet of Allah ﷺ travelled vast distances and stayed in Allah's company for thousands of years, and yet returned with his bed still warm, the water tap still flowing from ablution and the doorknocker still moving.

Ibrahim ﷺ, Yusuf ﷺ, and Sayyiduna Rasoolallah ﷺ were all helped by Allah through the means of Jibreel ﷺ. Allah decided to call upon Jibreel ﷺ as a means to protect and save His beloved prophets. Hence the Friends of Allah (*Awliya*) can and do help, which in reality is the help of Allah. This is not *Shirk*.

## Clarification

It is important to clarify a misunderstanding relating to the Prophet of Allah ﷺ and what happened to him in the Battle of Uhud. The Messenger of Allah ﷺ did not lose his blessed tooth in battle as commonly thought. His tooth was chipped. If the Prophet of Allah ﷺ were to have lost a tooth then this would have been an imperfection on his part, which is impossible for him. There can be no fault or deficiency in Allah's most beloved creation. The scholars of Hadith say that his tooth was chipped on the right side. His lip was cut which caused the bleeding (*Bukhari*). The person responsible for wounding the Prophet of Allah ﷺ was Utba bin Abu Waqas. The punishment inflicted on him for harming the Prophet of Allah ﷺ was that from his progeny (offspring) every child grew up toothless (*Al Mawahib al-Laduniyya*). Be warned! The enemies of the Prophet of

Allah ﷻ are cursed in this world and in the hereafter.

# Jibreel علیہ السلام & Mary

One day, Mary was sitting alone when Jibreel علیہ السلام descended in the form of a human. Mary was startled and asked "Who are you and what do you want?" He replied: "Do not be scared, Allah has sent me to bless you with a pure son. She replied that "How can I possibly give birth to a child when I am not married and no man has come near me?" Jibreel علیہ السلام said: "Allah has decided that a child can be born without a father. This is not difficult for Him. Allah to show His power has decided that a child will be born to you in such a manner." When Mary heard this, she was convinced. By Allah's will, Mary became pregnant. Allah says in the Holy Qur'an,

> '...Then We breathed into her of Our spirit (*Ruh*) and made her and her son a sign for the world.'
>
> *(Sura Maryam)*

The blessed and honourable institution of prophethood began with Adam علیہ السلام and it ended with Jesus son of Mary and our Beloved Prophet ﷺ came as the seal of all Prophets. Prophethood has been bestowed upon men not women. Hence Allah says in the Qur'an:

**'And We sent not before you [as messengers] except men...'**
*(12:109)*

That is why the circle of messengers started with a pure man and from that pure man, a pure woman was created. Adam ﷺ is the pure man and Eve was created from him. On completion of the circle of messengers, a pure man was created from a pure woman. From the pure Mary, pure Isa ﷺ was created without a father so that the circle of messengers beginning and end is joined together. The beginning and ending of prophethood was unique. This is why Allah says in the Qur'an:

**'The likeness of Jesus with Allah is like Adam. He created him of dust then said: "Be" and he was at once.'**
*(3:59)*

Adam's ﷺ composition was made of earth. That is why he descended from the heavens to the earth. Jesus son of Mary ﷺ on the other hand had the spirit breathed into him, which was heavenly, and hence why he was raised alive towards the heavens. Again we can see the likeness of Jesus ﷺ with that of Adam ﷺ.

It is abundantly clear from the verses of the Holy Qur'an and the sayings of the Messenger of Allah ﷺ that Jesus son of Mary عليه السلام was made from the spirit of Jibreel عليه السلام and his physical attributes are from his mother Mary. His physical and apparent appearance was human but his reality was angelic. Allah Almighty says in the Holy Qur'an:

> '...The Messiah Jesus son of Mary is only the Messenger of Allah and His word that was sent to Mary and a spirit from Him...'
>
> *(4:171)*

Hence Jesus son of Mary عليه السلام is a Word of Allah. Just as in a word there is a hidden meaning similarly in the body of the Messiah there is a thing that is hidden. And as Allah has called Jesus son of Mary "a spirit from Him" - and it is the job of the spirit to bring alive those things that touch it - that Allah gave him the miracle of bringing the dead back alive. We now understand the miracle of Jesus when he says:

> 'Indeed I have come to you with a sign from your Lord in that I design for you from clay [that which is] like the form of a bird, then I breathe into it and it becomes a bird by permission of Allah.'
>
> *(3:49)*

So we have established that the essence of Jesus son of Mary عليه السلام is twofold. One heavenly linked to Sayyiduna Jibreel عليه السلام the other earthly with Mary. Hence it is only appropriate that he spends some time in this world but also time in the heavens. It is custom that if someone is born outside of the country or region where their parents come from then after a short while they are taken to their original home so they are familiarised with their real surroundings and their family background. Similarly with Jesus ﷺ it was necessary for him to see his angelic and heavenly abode having already spent time in his worldly surroundings. After spending time in the heavens he will return to his worldly home and live a life by marrying and having children. Because he has the Word within him he did not marry and have children before his ascent. And because he is made of soil he will return back to earth and die like other human beings. He like all prophets before him and all of mankind will taste death and he will be buried next to the Final Messenger ﷺ in Madinah. Jesus ﷺ was born to Mary but has the spirit of Jibreel ﷺ inside him. Jibreel's ﷺ exaltation and his role in the revelation of Allah's words to His messengers is mentioned in the following ways:

**'The angels and Jibreel ascend towards Him.'**

*(70:4)*

**'Therein descend angels and Jibreel (the Spirit).'**

*(97:4)*

We learn from this that his ascent to the heavens and descent back to earth would have to take place at least once so that his unique position and status of having the Word in him be known. Just as Jibreel ﷺ has been called the *Ruh* so too has Jesus ﷺ.

> **'His word that was sent to Mary and a spirit from Him.'**
> *(4: 171)*

Hence just as the *Ruh*, namely Jibreel ﷺ, has had an ascent and descent so too in the same manner will Jesus return very soon to the world because Jesus ﷺ is a Spirit from Allah. It was impossible for the Jews to have killed him because it is impossible to kill a *Ruh*. Hence the verse of the Qur'an quoted above. Furthermore Allah Almighty says:

> **'...Towards Him ascends all pure words and the righteous work does He exalt...'**
> *(35:10)*

Hence why the raising to the heavens was appropriate and which has been proved in this story.

## Noor in human clothing

This story highlights that Jibreel ﷺ, an angel, appeared before Mary as a fit and healthy human being. In describing his appearance before Mary, Allah Almighty says in the Holy Qur'an:

'...and he appeared before her in the shape of healthy man.'
*(19:17)*

Now if someone were to say that Jibreel ﷺ is just like us then this would be sheer stupidity. Similarly, to say that Prophet Muhammad ﷺ is someone just like us and is like an elder brother is a severe insult to him.

## Real and figurative attributes

Jibreel ﷺ said to Mary:

'I am only a messenger of your Lord.
That I may give you a pure son.'
*(19:19)*

Whereas in reality it is Allah the creator who gives, Allah says in the Holy Qur'an:

'...He bestows daughters on whomsoever He likes and He bestows sons on whomsoever He likes.'

*(26:49)*

In the latter verse the operative word is that Allah gives. And in the previous verse Jibreel ﷺ says that he gives. Is there not a contradiction between these two verses of the Holy Qur'an? No, not at all. There is no contradiction here or anywhere else in the Qur'an. In the latter verse the nature of giving is real (*Haqeeqi*) whereas the giving of Jibreel ﷺ to Mary is metaphorical (*Mujaazi*). The reality is that Allah gives in all cases and scenarios but the giving is attributed to others. It was Allah, the Creator and Sustainer of the whole universe, that gave Mary a child, but the way and means Allah gave this child was through Jibreel ﷺ. Hence Jibreel ﷺ said to Mary that I have come to you to give you a child even though in reality it was from Allah.

Examples of this can be found in our daily lives. A doctor giving medicine that makes someone better, or a doctor prescribing something that makes someone worse, not better. Eating something that causes an upset stomach and then taking something to make it better. The question in all these scenarios are is it the doctor making us better or worse through the medicine or is it Allah? Is the pain caused in the stomach from Allah or from the food, and is the relief from Allah or from the medication? It is Allah who makes us better but it is through the doctor and his medication that we find cures and relief. And it is Allah's will that from the medication we get better or worse. We find other instances where expressions are made to similar affect. If someone says that their son is "pir baksh" they mean that Allah bestowed them a child with the prayers of a Shaykh or Wali when all other modes failed. When we say that Maula Ali is *'Mushkil Kusha'* (remover of difficulties) by this we mean that Allah relieves our difficulties by the means of Maula Ali because Allah loves him and he loves Allah. But there are some who cannot comprehend this concept and accuse Muslims of *Kufr* and *Shirk*.

From this story we also learn that when Jibreel ﷺ took the soul from Allah he was in his angelic form but when he appeared before Mary he took a human appearance. He was *Noor* in Allah's presence taking the *Ruh* but human in giving it to Mary. Similarly the *Haqeeqat* (real essence) of our Prophet ﷺ is that he is *Noor* and as it is stated that Allah is the provider and he is the distributor (*Qasim*). He is *Noor* in Allah's presence when receiving and he is human when he is giving to his Ummah. If the Prophet of Allah ﷺ was not *Noor* how could he receive from Allah? Furthermore if he was not *Noor* then how could the Miraj take place? And if he was not human then how could he return to earth?

# Revelation of the Qur'an took one of two forms

Imam Jalaluddin Suyuti, may Allah be pleased with him, says that the revelation of the Holy Qur'an took one of two forms. One is that the Holy Prophet ﷺ discarded his human appearance and took on his *Noori* appearance to receive the revelation from Jibreel عليه السلام who was also in his *Noori* and angelic form. Or Jibreel عليه السلام used to come with the revelation in human form to the Prophet of Allah ﷺ who was also in his blessed and perfect human appearance (*al-Itqaan*). So at the time of revelation either the Prophet of Allah ﷺ changed appearance or Jibreel عليه السلام changed appearance to receive the words of Allah. In both scenarios it does not change the fact that the reality of Jibreel عليه السلام is that he is *Noor* but can take human form and that above all, the Messenger and Beloved of Allah ﷺ is *Noor* and he took human appearance as the Final Messenger.

*Bashr bun kar khuda ka noor aya*
*Humein Qur'an haqq suna kar aya*

The light of Allah came as a human
To teach us the Qur'an the truth

• 7 •

# The Hadith of Jibreel عَلَيْهِ السَّلَام

Sayyiduna Umar ؓ said: "While we were sitting with the Messenger of Allah ﷺ, one day a man came up to us whose clothes were extremely white, whose hair was extremely black, upon whom traces of travelling could not be seen, and whom none of us knew, until he sat down close to the Prophet ﷺ, so that he rested his knees touching his knees and placed his two hands upon his thighs and said: 'Muhammad ﷺ, tell me about Islam.' The Messenger of Allah ﷺ, said: 'Islam is that you witness that there is no God but Allah and that Muhammad is the Messenger of Allah, and you establish the prayer, and you give the Zakat, and you fast Ramadan, and you perform the Hajj of the House of Allah if you are able to take a path to it.' He said: 'You have told the truth.' We were amazed at him asking him and then telling him that he told the truth. He said: 'Tell me about Iman.' He said: 'That you have belief in Allah, His angels, His books, His messengers, and the Last Day, and that you affirm the Destiny, the good of it and the bad of it.'

He said: 'You have told the truth.' He said: 'Tell me about Ihsan.' He said: 'That you worship Allah as if you see Him, for if you do not see Him then truly He sees you.' He said: 'Tell me about the Hour [Day of Judgement].' He said: 'The one asked about it knows no more than the one asking.' He said: 'Then tell me about its signs.' He said: 'That the female slave should give birth to her mistress and you see poor, naked, barefoot shepherds of sheep and goats competing in making tall buildings.' He went away, and I remained some time. Then the Prophet of Allah ﷺ asked: 'Umar ؓ, do you know who the questioner was?' I said: 'Allah and His Messenger know best.' He said: 'He was Jibreel ؑ who came to you to teach you your religion."

*(Mishkat Sharif)*

Jibreel ؑ, an angel, came and taught us the religion not in his own appearance but that of a man. The Companions present were fortunate to learn the religion and see Jibreel ؑ. They saw him in splendid white clothes and with dark black hair. But the reality of Jibreel ؑ is that he is made out of *Noor* (divine light). He is an angel. In this instance he was dressed as a human being. If we can accept the fact that Jibreel ؑ a creature made of light can appear in the form of a human being to teach the religion, then it is not difficult to accept that the Prophet of Allah ﷺ whose existence and being is of *Noor* came to us in the form of a perfect human being and came to teach us the religion.

Jibreel ﷺ sat in front of the Prophet of Allah ﷺ in such a way just as a person sits in Prayer. Jibreel ﷺ teaches us that the respect needed for the Prophet of Allah ﷺ is the same needed when we present ourselves to Allah.

# Islam

Jibreel ﷺ asked the Prophet of Allah ﷺ about Islam. The Prophet of Allah ﷺ told him that it is you witness that there is no God but Allah and that Muhammad ﷺ is the Messenger of Allah, and you establish the Prayer, and you give the Zakat, and you fast Ramadan, and you perform the Hajj of the House if you are able to take a path to it. All these actions will be accepted and of benefit if one has Iman (faith). If there is no faith, then there is no value in Prayer and fasting and Zakat and Hajj. If you see people who pray and make other people pray, and go on *Tabligh* and knock on people's doors and make them pray and so on, but do not have the true conviction of faith inside them, then their actions are futile.

# Iman

Jibreel ﷺ then asked the Prophet of Allah ﷺ what Iman was. The Prophet of Allah ﷺ replied 'that you have belief in Allah, His angels, His books, His messengers, and the Last Day, and that you affirm the Destiny, the good of it and the bad of it.'

We learn then from the Prophet of Allah ﷺ that belief in Allah alone is not enough. This is not Iman. We have to believe in His angels, books, Prophets, Judgement Day and fate; otherwise you are lacking in faith. Molvi Ismail Dehlvi in *Taqwiyatul Iman* disagrees. He says that "Believe in Allah and nothing else." What ignorance on the part of Ismail Dehlvi to say to believe only in Allah and Him alone when the words of the Prophet of Allah ﷺ on the questioning of Jibreel ﷺ clearly states that Iman is to believe in Allah *and* His angels, books, Prophets, Judgement Day and fate. Who are we to believe, Ismail Dehlvi or the Beloved Messenger of Allah ﷺ?

## *Ihsan*

The Prophet of Allah ﷺ was then asked about *Ihsan*. He said *Ihsan* was "that you worship Allah as if you see Him, for if you do not see Him then truly He sees you." *Ihsan* is a very high status and can only be reached by the friends of Allah. The purpose of the Prophet's ﷺ statement is to place a sense of *Taqwa* (fear of Allah) into people's hearts and minds. Because if we start to think of Allah that we are seeing Him or that He is seeing us in worship this mentality will carry on when we are not praying and that sense of the Divine Presence is always there. In short *Ihsan* creates sincerity (*Ikhlas*) in worship.

## Knowledge of the Day of Judgement

Jibreel عليه السلام then asked the Prophet ﷺ about the Day of Judgement. The Prophet of Allah ﷺ said: "The one asked about it knows no more than the one asking." The Prophet of Allah ﷺ did not say "I do not know" to mean that he did not have the knowledge of the Final Hour. The Prophet of Allah's ﷺ statement should be seen that he has knowledge; otherwise he would have never responded to Jibreel عليه السلام by telling him the signs of the Final Hour. If he did not have knowledge of the Day of Judgement then how could he describe its signs! If you do not know the name of something how can you go on to describe it? For example if I asked someone "do you know Zaid?" and that person says no, then it would be sheer stupidity to go on and ask the features and characteristics of Zaid.

The Hadith proves that the Prophet of Allah ﷺ does have knowledge of the Final Hour but decided not to disclose this knowledge to Jibreel ﷺ. Why? Allah says in the Qur'an:

'Surely the Hour is to come, I like to keep it concealed so that everyone maybe rewarded for what he strives for.'
*(20:15)*

'...the sudden overtaking of the Last Hour without their perceiving it at all?'
*(12:107)*

'And those who disbelieve will ever remain in doubt about it until the Hour comes upon them suddenly...'
*(22:55)*

The Day of Judgement has been hidden so that mankind is fearful of its coming. This sense of fear for Allah is meant to make us more pious and conscious of Allah Almighty. Similarly the time of our death is hidden from us. Death can come to us at any time and at any place. The Day of Judgement is a certainty. Allah has kept this knowledge exclusively to Himself so that the Hour is without warning and sudden. If the timing of the Final Hour was disclosed then it would not be sudden and without warning. This is why the Prophet of Allah ﷺ did not disclose the timing of the Hour to Jibreel ﷺ. Knowledge of the Hour is amongst the Divine secrets.

# The Prophet's ﷺ knowledge of the Day of Judgement

Sayyiduna Hudhayfa ؓ says:

'The Prophet ﷺ stood among us [speaking] for a long time and did not leave out one thing from that time until the rising of the Final Hour except he told us about it. Whoever remembered it remembered it and whoever forgot it forgot it. All those who are present know this. Some of it I might have forgotten, then I see it [happen] and remember it just as someone would remember a man who had been away and then appears before him and he instantly recognises him.'
*(Bukhari & Muslim)*

Amr ibn Aktab al-Ansari ؓ says:

'The Prophet of Allah ﷺ prayed Fajr with us then climbed the pulpit and addressed us until the time came for Zuhr, then he descended and prayed. Then he climbed the pulpit and addressed us until the time came for Asr, whereupon he descended and prayed. Then he climbed the pulpit and addressed us until the sun set. He informed us about all that was to happen until the Day of Resurrection. The most knowledgeable of us is he who has memorised the most.'
*(Sahih Muslim)*

These two narrations show that the Prophet of Allah ﷺ had knowledge of everything from the beginning till the Day of Judgement. It is self-evident that when the world ends the Day of Judgement will start thereafter. If he did not have God-given knowledge of the Final Hour, then how could he transmit such knowledge to his Companions?

Sayyiduna Jibreel asked the Prophet of Allah ﷺ about the signs of the Final Hour. The Prophet of Allah ﷺ told him that the slave girl would control the master. One interpretation of this is that children will disrespect their parents. The words of our Prophet ﷺ are true as we see today children disrespecting their parents. The second thing the Prophet of Allah ﷺ said was that barefooted, naked shepherds will boast and compete in constructing tall buildings. We need to go no further than Riyadh and Dubai where barefooted Arabs boast about their skyscrapers and palaces. The Prophet of Allah's ﷺ words are absolutely true.

# Jibreel عليه السلام, the Prophet's ﷺ *Wazir* (Minister)

The Prophet of Allah ﷺ said: "I have two *Wazirs* (ministers) on the earth and two in the heavens. The *Wazir* of the heavens are Jibreel عليه السلام and Mikaeel عليه السلام and the two *Wazirs* of the earth are Abu Bakr رضي الله عنه and Umar رضي الله عنه."

*(Mishkat Sharif)*

It is self-evident that ministers are people of power and authority. The authority and jurisdiction of the minister is a reflection of the leader they serve. Jibreel عليه السلام and Mikaeel عليه السلام are the Prophet's ﷺ ministers in the heavens, while Abu Bakr رضي الله عنه and Umar رضي الله عنه are the Prophet's ﷺ ministers on the earth. That means that the Prophet of Allah ﷺ is king of both worlds. He is *Sayyidus Saqalayn*. On the night of Miraj, the Prophet of Allah ﷺ made an "official visit" to his other realm of authority which is the heavens. The Prophet of Allah ﷺ was informing his Ummah on earth that his authority spans both domains. A king's minister always has the power and authority to do something. It can never be that someone is appointed a minister and have no power and authority. Politicians today vie for ministerial position because they know that the post has responsibilities and benefits with it. If being a minister meant not having power and authority then politicians would not vie for it. Any power that a minister has is given to them and the person that gives them this power is their leader. But Molvi Ismail Dehlvi in *Taqwiyatul Iman* states: "Whoever is named Muhammad or Ali has no authority over anything." The Prophet of Allah ﷺ by inference of this Hadith from *Mishkat Sharif* states that he is powerful and authoritative yet a scholar from the 19$^{th}$ century thinks otherwise. Should we believe Allah's Prophet ﷺ or Molvi Ismail?

## The Prophet of Allah ﷺ is *Hakim* (Ruler)

Allah Almighty in the Qur'an says to his beloved Prophet ﷺ:

'Then, O beloved! By your Lord, they shall not be
Muslims until they make you judge in all disputes among
themselves, then they find no impediments in their hearts
concerning whatever you decide,
and accept from the core of their hearts.'

*(4:65)*

To be a true Muslim it is necessary to regard the Prophet of Allah ﷺ as *Hakim* and as we know a *Hakim* cannot be without power and authority. A *Hakim* by definition is powerful and authoritative. A *Hakim* has total control over his dominion and retains full control. We have to understand that Allah Almighty, the ultimate and real *Hakim* is calling His Beloved Prophet ﷺ a *Hakim*. Allah Almighty has entrusted His Prophet ﷺ with this power and authority. So anyone who does not acknowledge the Prophet of Allah ﷺ in the light of this verse of the Holy Qur'an is denying the Qur'an and the Prophet ﷺ, and thus is not a true Muslim, no matter how pious they may seem to be.

## The Prophet of Allah ﷺ is *Mukhtar* (Independent)

The Prophet of Allah ﷺ is a Prophet and Mercy for the entire creation and he is the *Hakim* of it. Whatever he wishes and says is law and has to be obeyed and respected. He is the commander of the Shariah. This authority and power is not his own. It is from Allah, Who says in the Holy Qur'an:

> '...He makes lawful to them clean and pure things and prohibits them from things that are impure...'
> *(5:157)*

In this verse Allah has given the Prophet of Allah ﷺ the authority to make things lawful and prohibited and to make things pure and impure. Allah declares in the following verse those things that are Haram:

'Forbidden to you for food are dead meat (carrion) and blood and the flesh of swine and that on which a name other than Allah has been invoked, and that which dies by strangling or is dead because of injury or by falling from a height or is gored to death or eaten by a wild animal unless you find it still alive and slaughter it yourselves...'

*(5:3)*

The Holy Qur'an lists four things that are classified as Haram. There is no mention at all of dogs, donkeys, jackals, snakes, lizards and a whole host of other harmful animals. Furthermore there is no mention of urine or excrement or other toxic and harmful materials. In the Holy Qur'an you will not find reference to anything else other than the four categories as being classified as Haram. So are these things mentioned above permissible to be consumed? No. This is because Allah also states in the Holy Qur'an:

'...And whatever the Holy Messenger gives you take it and what he forbids, abstain from it...'

*(59:7)*

To know what else is Halal and what is Haram, we must refer to the Sunnah. If we did not then we would consume food and drink that would be impure and harmful for us. If Allah Almighty wanted He could have easily listed all the Haram things in the Qur'an. But instead of doing that He decided to raise the status of His Beloved even further by giving him the authority to declare what was Halal and what was Haram. The Prophet of Allah ﷺ said:

> 'The Qur'an was given to me and with it a likeness (i.e. my sayings -Hadith) Beware! Indeed soon there will be a man with a full belly sitting in his chair saying 'just look at Qur'an. What it says is Halal is Halal and what it says is Haram is Haram'. When in actual fact whatever your Prophet makes Haram is just as if Allah has made it Haram. Your domesticated donkey is unlawful for you and so are your birds and animals.'
>
> *(Mishkat Sharif)*

The Prophet of Allah's ﷺ prohibition of these things holds the same weight as if Allah Himself declared these things Haram. Now for those Muslims who *only* use Qur'an as a proof, who disregard the Sunnah and believe that the Messenger of Allah ﷺ is a being without power and authority they should go ahead and eat rats, dogs and donkey meat.

## The Prophet of Allah ﷺ made impure things Haram

Before the Prophet of Allah ﷺ would go to the toilet he would supplicate by saying: "O Allah! I seek refuge from the impure things."

Among the many things Allah says in the Holy Qur'an about the status of the Holy Prophet ﷺ is that he makes "impure things unlawful." People who reject the authority of the Prophet ﷺ and the value of his sayings should think again when they go to clean themselves in the toilet.

Infinite blessings and salutations upon the Prophet of Allah ﷺ who made for his Ummah things pure to consume and benefit from. And furthermore he made impure things unlawful so that our lives are not harmed in any way. You will find people in the world today who eat dogs, snakes, snails and other impure animals. Indeed they are regarded as delicacies and are a lucrative market in some countries. In China, for example, the people there eat mice, snakes and crocodiles. The French people are known to eat snails. Some people in India drink their own urine and believe that they attain blessings from it. What an enormous favour the Final Messenger of Allah ﷺ has done on this Ummah that he has clarified for us those things that are pure and beneficial for us and those things that are impure and harmful for us. The Hadith recorded in *Mishkat* describes a likeness between the Holy Qur'an and Sunnah. The Prophet of Allah ﷺ describes his words and actions as a likeness to what the Qur'an orders. Allah says in the Holy Qur'an:

**'And if you have any doubt as to what We have sent down upon our exalted servant then bring just one chapter like it and call upon all your helpers besides Allah if you are truthful.'**

*(2:23)*

Allah Almighty says in this verse that His Word is without likeness and yet His Beloved Messenger ﷺ says that his actions are a likeness to the Qur'an. There is an apparent contradiction between what Allah is saying and what His Prophet ﷺ is saying. This however is not the case. What Allah is saying in the Qur'an is in regards to the words, eloquence and authenticity of the Qur'an. Allah lays down the challenge to the polytheists to bring a likeness to it, a challenge they and all of humanity are doomed to fail in. The Prophet of Allah ﷺ calls his words and actions a likeness to the Qur'an not in terms of eloquence but in terms of authority because whatever the Prophet ﷺ has made Haram is as if Allah has made it Haram. So if something is termed lawful or forbidden in Hadith it carries the same weight and authority as if it was deemed lawful or forbidden in the Holy Qur'an. Hence this is why the Holy Prophet ﷺ said: "Whatever thing your Prophet makes Haram is just as if Allah has made it Haram…"

# Jibreel علیہ السلام the Prophet's ﷺ soldier

In the Battle of Badr the Messenger of Allah ﷺ said to Ibn Abbas: "Look! There is Jibreel علیہ السلام on his horse. His bridle is held back and he has a weapon in his hand."

*(Bukhari)*

'When the Messenger of Allah ﷺ returned from the Battle of the Trench and took off his armour and bathed, Jibreel علیہ السلام came to him and said: "O Prophet of Allah ﷺ! You have taken off your armour. By Allah! We have not taken off our armour. We are still equipped to fight. Come! We have to punish the Banu Quraiza for their treachery." So the Prophet ﷺ put on his armour and went with Jibreel علیہ السلام.'

*(Bukhari)*

In the Holy Qur'an Allah recalls the incident that took place with Prophet Ibrahim ﷺ:

> 'O my Apostle! Has the story of the honoured guests of Ibrahim reached you?'
>
> *(51:24)*

Allah sent some angels as guests to Ibrahim ﷺ. A host will always look after their guests whether they are better than them or not. A host does not look down and question their guests. Angels were the guests of Ibrahim and he hosted them. But when the chief of the angels appears in front of the chief of the Prophets ﷺ he comes not as a guest but as a servant, a soldier ready to fight.

Hence we find in the Holy Qur'an:

> '...Your Lord shall reinforce you with 5000 angels bearing marks of distinction'.
>
> *(3:125)*

> '...And besides all this, the angels are his helpers'.
>
> *(66:4)*

The Prophet of Allah ﷺ is Master not only for man and Jinn but for the angels too.

## Jibreel's ﷺ horse

Ibn Abbas ؓ says that in the Battle of Badr the Muslims were in pursuit of the enemies when the enemies were fleeing. All of a sudden from above their heads, they could hear the sound of horses and a voice saying "Ahead O Hayzum!"

Hayzum was the name of Jibreel's ﷺ horse. In the Battle of Badr the angels sent by Allah supported the believers. Companions reported that they went to attack the enemy when all of a sudden the enemy's head was chopped off. The Companions told the Prophet of Allah ﷺ of this strange occurrence to which the Messenger of Allah ﷺ replied: "This is help from the second heaven."

*(Tafsir Khazahinul Irfan)*

After the Battle of Badr Jibreel ﷺ in his full armour and horseback went to the Prophet of Allah ﷺ and said "Ya RasoolAllah! Allah has sent me here. He has ordered me not to leave your side till you are satisfied. O Prophet! Are you happy with me?" The Prophet ﷺ told him that he was happy. With this news Jibreel ﷺ sought the Prophet's ﷺ permission and left.

What more can be said about the high rank and status of our beloved Messenger ﷺ when Jibreel ﷺ, the chief of the angels, is his soldier and defender?

· 10 ·

# Jibreel ﷷ and the accursed Abu Jahl

One day Abu Jahl said to his friends that he would go and place a boulder on the head of Muhammad ﷺ while he was in prostration. Hence the next day Abu Jahl got a big stone and sat waiting for the Prophet ﷺ to appear for prayer. The Prophet of Allah ﷺ made his way to the Ka'bah and began praying. He ﷺ went into prostration when Abu Jahl was about to throw the stone on the Prophet's ﷺ head. Abu Jahl approached the Prophet ﷺ when all of a sudden he was frightened away by a sight that changed the colour of his face and made the boulder crumble into dust. He returned to his friends who asked him what had happened to him. Abu Jahl told them that as he approached the Prophet ﷺ a wild looking camel with a long neck and big sharp teeth said to me that if I took another step closer it would eat me alive. The Prophet of Allah ﷺ heard Abu Jahl's account and remarked "the camel that came to frighten him was

Jibreel ﷺ."

*(Jawahirul Bihaar)*

Jibreel ﷺ is the leader of the angels. He is a courtier of the Prophet's ﷺ *Darbar* (court) and it is his duty to protect the Prophet of Allah ﷺ at all times. Angels not only protect the Messenger of Allah ﷺ but they also protect his city- al Madinah al-Munawarrah. The Prophet of Allah ﷺ said: "In every corner of Madinah angels are keeping guard so that plagues and the Dajjal (Antichrist) cannot enter."

Why does Madinah have this status? The simple reason is because it is the city of the Beloved of Allah ﷺ. It is because of the holy presence of the Prophet ﷺ that angels protect the city so that plagues and the Dajjal cannot enter it.

## Madinah is free from Polytheism

Logical analysis of the Hadith indicates that a calamity much worse than plague - which is associating partners with Allah - cannot enter the city of the Prophet ﷺ. Plagues can take away lives but *Shirk* takes away faith. So how can it be that plague cannot enter Madinah but *Shirk* can? The fact is that Madinah is free from *Shirk*. The Wahhabi rulers however wrongly claim that *Shirk* prevails in the city of the Prophet ﷺ. They have used this as a lame excuse to obliterate the signs of Islam like the graveyard of Baqee and other historical landmarks of Madinah and Islam in the name of freeing Madinah of something that cannot exist there in the first place. The Messenger of Allah ﷺ said: "I do not fear my Ummah committing polytheism but I fear my Ummah will be inclined towards the world." (*Mishkat, Bukhari*)

The Prophet of Allah ﷺ who has knowledge about his Ummah's actions made it crystal clear that he has no fear whatsoever of his followers attributing partners to Allah but feared that his followers would be trapped into futile worldly pursuits. The Messenger of Allah ﷺ is absolutely right in this regard. We Muslims are sinners. We acknowledge our weaknesses and ask Allah for forgiveness. But we are not polytheists as some groups claim. How can we be polytheists when the Prophet of Allah ﷺ has said that he was not concerned for his followers for committing such a heinous crime after him?

Imam Ahmad Raza Khan Bareilwi wrote:

> *Shirk thehre jis mein ta'zeem-e Habeeb*
> *Us bureh mazhab pe laanat kijiye*

> **For honour (*Ta'zeem*) of the Beloved they call it polytheism**
> **Send curses on that dreadful sect!**

# • 11 •

# Jibreel علیہ السلام and the green silk suit

'Jibreel علیہ السلام appeared before the Messenger of Allah ﷺ with a green silk suit that had an image of Aisha bint Abu Bakr رضی اللہ عنہا on it. He showed it to the Prophet of Allah ﷺ and said, "She is to be your wife in this world and in the hereafter."'

*(Mishkat Sharif)*

'For three consecutive nights he appeared before the Prophet ﷺ with this green suit. The Prophet of Allah ﷺ said "O Aisha! Jibreel علیہ السلام has been bringing your image to me on a suit. This marriage is from Allah and will remain so."'

*(Mishkat Sharif)*

Jibreel's علیہ السلام dispatching of the green silk suit to the Prophet ﷺ was the command of Allah. We learn from these sayings that the marriage of Aisha رضی اللہ عنہا to the Prophet ﷺ was the will of Allah. Fathers, grandfathers, uncles, or family friends help decide marital relations but in the case of Sayyida Aisha رضی اللہ عنہا, Allah Almighty arranged her marriage with His Beloved.

## Jibreel ﷺ sends salutations to Aisha

'The Messenger of Allah ﷺ said, "O Aisha! Here is Jibreel ﷺ sending his Salaams upon you." Aisha then replied back to Jibreel ﷺ.'

*(Mishkat Sharif)*

Ala Hazrat Imam Ahmad Raza Khan Bareilwi says in his famous Salaam "Mustafa Jaan-e-Rahmat":

*Bint Siddiq Aaram jaan Nabi*
*Us Hareem Bara'at peh lahkon salaam*

*Daughter of Siddiq, the comfort of the Prophet*
*A million salutations on that sanctuary of freedom*

*Ya'nee hai sura Noor jinki gawah*
*unki purnoor soorat peh lahko salaam*

Sura Noor is a witness to her purity
A million salutations on her face of spiritual light

## Sura Noor

When the hypocrites raised allegations against Aisha, Allah responded to their idle talk. This is because He wanted to refute their baseless allegations against a marriage that He sanctioned. Sura Noor was revealed which protected her chastity and honour against the great allegation made against her.

Allah Almighty says in the Qur'an:

> 'And why it did not so happen, when you heard it you would have said, "It is not befitting to us to speak about such thing? Allah hollowed be, You this is a great slander.'
>
> *(24:16)*

> 'Dirty women are for dirty men and dirty men are for dirty women and clean women are for clean men and clean men are for clean women they are free from what they are saying. For them is forgiveness and an honourable provision.'
>
> *(24:26)*

In the latter verse Allah has made it unequivocally clear that for the pure people there will only be pure things. So how could this marriage be impure?

## Clothes

Allah Almighty says in Sura al-Baqara:

> 'They (women) are a clothing for you and you are a clothing for them.'
>
> *(2:187)*

Furthermore Allah says in the Qur'an:

> 'And keep clean your clothes.'
>
> *(74:4)*

Hence whoever stains the reputation of Sayyida Aisha ﷺ has stained the reputation of the Holy Prophet of Allah ﷺ and this indeed is a dreadful thing to do.

## *Muzakki*

Among the many names and attributes Allah has bestowed upon His Beloved Messenger ﷺ is the name of *Muzakki* which means one who purifies others.

Allah Almighty says in the Holy Qur'an:

> '[Allah]...Sent a Messenger who recites unto them His signs and purifies them...'
>
> *(3:164)*

The result of people keeping the company of Prophet Muhammad ﷺ is that he made ill-mannered people the most mannered people. He turned the ignorant and arrogant into the most knowledgeable, humble and wise. He turned the impure and dirty people into clean and pure people. The fortunate people who spent time in the company of the Holy Prophet ﷺ even for a short space of time benefited immensely from it. So how could it possibly be that the person that arguably spent the most time in his presence be denied the blessings of being purified? The *Tazkiya* - purification - indeed reached his wives as well as all the Companions (may Allah be pleased with them all). This is why when Allah calls His Prophet ﷺ *Tayyib*, then for him there can only be *Tayyiba*.

# Mother

Allah Almighty in the Holy Qur'an has described the wives of the Prophet ﷺ as the 'Mother of the Believers':

> 'This Prophet is closer to the Muslims even more than their own selves and his wives are their mothers..."
> 
> *(33:6)*

Why does Allah call the wives of the Prophet ﷺ the 'mother of the believers'? The reason is because the mother is a relation of respect and honour. To swear and dishonour your mother is a sign of disgrace and humiliation. Allah says in the Qur'an:

> '...Utter not even a faint cry to them and chide them not and speak to them the word of respect.'
> 
> *(17:23)*

So how unfortunate are those people who swear and dishonour their spiritual mother Sayyida Aisha?

# Mother of the Believers

Sayyida Fatima ؏, the Lady of Paradise has a great rank and status in Islam. The Prophet of Allah ﷺ said to her: "O Fatima!

Would you not be happy being the leader of the heavenly women and the believing women?" (*Mishkat Sharif*)

According to this Hadith, Sayyida Fatima is the leader of believing women but not for believing men. But Allah has made the wives of the Prophet ﷺ the mothers of all believers. So in this respect Sayyida Aisha holds an honour above Sayyida Fatima of being mother to both believing men and women.

## Sayyida Aisha - Hadith Scholar and Jurist

Sayyida Aisha ؓ was a great narrator of Hadith and a great jurist. Abu Musa ؓ says that when they wanted to understand a Hadith of the Holy Prophet ﷺ which they could not understand, they would go to Sayyida Aisha ؓ because she understood the Hadith best and could resolve their difficulties. (*Mishkat Sharif*)

# Food at Sayyida Aisha's

Imam-e-Rabbani Shaykh Ahmad Sirhindi, may Allah be pleased with him, says in his *Maktubaat*:

"For many years it has been my way to cook some food (*Niyaz*) and offer its reward to the soul of the Messenger of Allah ﷺ and to Sayyiduna Ali, Imam Hasan, Imam Hussain and Sayyida Fatima (may Allah be pleased with them all). One year when I did this, the Holy Prophet ﷺ appeared in my dream. I said my salaams to him but he did not pay attention towards me so I asked him what the matter was? The Prophet of Allah ﷺ said: "I eat my food at (Sayyida) Aisha's. If you want to send reward to me then do it at Aisha's." At that moment I realised that when I sent the reward I forgot to mention her. After that I always included her name in particular along with the wives of the Prophet ﷺ whenever I cooked *Niyaz* and performed *Fatiha* on their souls as they too are part of the Ahle Bayt."

We learn from this story of Shaykh Sirhindi, may Allah be pleased with him, that the Prophet of Allah ﷺ was not happy with him because he forgot to mention Sayyida Aisha despite remembering the rest of the Ahle Bayt. This is because the Prophet of Allah ﷺ ate at the house of Aisha. Shaykh Sirhindi understood his mistake and rectified it straight away.

## Offering *Fatiha* is not an innovation

It is proved from *Maktubaat Sharif* of Shaykh Sirhindi, may Allah be pleased with him, that to prepare *Niyaz* and to offer *Fatiha* for the souls of the pious is permissible and indeed encouraged. It is not an innovation of misguidance. If offering *Fatiha* in the way Shaykh Sirhindi did were a reprehensible act then the Prophet of Allah ﷺ would have reprimanded his actions. Indeed the Prophet of Allah ﷺ came into his dream to make his actions complete by telling him that he will be happy with his deeds if he remembered his beloved wife Sayyida Aisha. Groups critical of our practices and ways should acknowledge Shaykh Ahmad Sirhindi's words and accept his ruling that *Fatiha* is permissible.

## Allah wishes the happiness of His Beloved

We conclude the analysis of this story by reflecting on the pure *Aqidah* of our mother Sayyida Aisha ؓ when she said to the Beloved of Allah ﷺ "Your Lord is quick in making you happy" (*Bukhari*). In other words whatever he wishes Allah fulfils it. Now let us compare this to the opinion of Molvi Ismail Dehlvi who said in *Taqwiyatul Iman* "what happens from the

Prophet's wanting?" i.e. nothing (God Forbid). In short Molvi Ismail's opinions and that of the scholars of Deoband is the exact opposite of the beliefs of the Faithful, Sayyida Aisha ﷺ and all the true followers of Islam. Our belief should be firm and pure just like our Mother Sayyida Aisha and not one that is defective and insulting like that of Molvi Ismail and the scholars of Deoband.

*Khuda ki raza chahata hein doh alam*
*Khuda chahata hein raza e Muhammad* ﷺ

**The creation wishes the *Rida* (happiness) of its Lord**
**The Lord wises the *Rida* of Muhammad** ﷺ

• 12 •

# Sayyiduna Ali & Jibreel ﷻ

Sayyiduna Ali ﷺ once said: "Ask me about the pathways of the heavens because I know them better than I know the pathways of the earth." At that moment Sayyiduna Jibreel ﷻ appeared in the form of a man and asked Ali that if his claim was true then he should tell him immediately the whereabouts of Jibreel ﷻ. He lifted his head towards the skies and looked left and right. He then looked towards the ground and looked left and right. He then said to the stranger: "I looked for Jibreel ﷻ in the heavens and he was not there. I looked on the earth he was not there either. Therefore I say that you are Jibreel ﷻ."

*(Nuzhatul Majaalis)*

Maulana Jalaluddin Rumi says in his Masnawi *"Lawh Mahfooz Ast pesh Awliya"* which means that the Preserved Tablet is always in sight of the Friends of Allah. What is the Preserved Tablet?

Allah says in the Qur'an:

> 'And there is not any grain in the darkness of the earth,
> and nor anything wet and nor dry
> which is not written in a Luminous Book.'
>
> (6:59)

In other words the whole world is in front of the *Awliya*. Sayyiduna Ali is *Sayyidul Awliya* – the Leader of the *Awliya*. So how could it be that something is hidden from his sight? Sayyiduna Ali's status and rank is immensely great but he is a slave to his master, Prophet Muhammad. In the light of this Hadith can the knowledge of the Prophet of Allah be comprehended? If the Messenger of Allah's loyal servant Sayyiduna Ali knows the whereabouts of the leader of angels, can anything then be hidden from the Master of both worlds? But despite this some ignorant and misleading people say that the Prophet of Allah has no knowledge of what is behind a wall. This statement was made in *Baraheen Qaati'a* by Rashid Ahmad Gangohi- the revered Deobandi Scholar. Are we to believe Gangohi or the Leader of all the Prophets and Messengers?

• 13 •

# Jibreel علیہ السلام, Mikaeel and the camel

Sayyiduna Ali left his house one day with some cotton thread his wife Sayyida Fatima gave him to sell in the market so they could buy some flour. Ali sold the thread for six dirhams. With this money he went to buy some goods when he came across a person seeking his help. Ali gave him the money instead. After a short while a stranger appeared with a very healthy and beautiful looking camel. He asked Ali if he wanted to buy it. Ali told him that he was tempted but did not have the money. The stranger nevertheless gave Ali the camel and went away. Soon after another stranger came and asked Ali whether he would sell the camel? The man took the camel off Ali for three hundred dirhams. Ali after that went in search for the first man but could not find him and went home. He arrived at home to see that the Holy Prophet was there. The Prophet said to Ali, 'will you tell us about the incident with the camel or shall I?' Ali respectfully asked the Prophet ﷺ to tell the story. The Prophet ﷺ told Fatima and Ali that the first man was no ordinary stranger but was Jibreel عليه السلام and the second stranger was Mikaeel عليه السلام and that the camel was from heaven on which Sayyida Fatima will ride on the Day of Judgement. The Prophet of Allah ﷺ told Ali that Allah loved his compassion to the person seeking his help so much that Jibreel عليه السلام and Mikaeel عليه السلام came to show you some of your reward in Paradise.

*(Nuzhatul Majaalis)*

To give charity (*sadaqa*) and to respond to the requests of the needy makes Allah Almighty exceedingly happy. Allah rewards such charitable people with immense benefits and blessings in this world and in the hereafter. The Prophet of Allah ﷺ said:

**"Whoever aids his brother Allah assists him and whoever removes a difficulty of a Muslim on the Day of Judgement Allah will remove that person's problems."**

*(Mishkat Sharif)*

From this Hadith we are instructed to help and assist our fellow Muslims. Furthermore we have been asked to help remove the difficulties of other Muslims. It is incumbent upon us to assist someone in their troubles.

## Allah's friends by His leave are removers of difficulties

From this Hadith we also learn that by Allah's permission people can aid needy people and be remover of difficulties. The word used in the Hadith is *Farraja*, which is derived from the word *Faraj* that means 'opening'. The word *Kurbatun* used in the Hadith means difficulty or problem. So whoever helps his fellow Muslim in this world, in return Allah will assist them on the Day of Judgement. The word *Kushaa* is Persian which also means to open or resolve. Hence it is proved that Allah's friends by His permission are removers of difficulties.

## An angel in human form

Sayyiduna Jibreel ﷺ and Mikaeel ﷺ both appeared not in their angelic and natural form but as human beings. Now if someone was to attribute humanness to them then this would be a very foolish thing to do because even though they appeared to be human, their nature is in actual fact angelic and made of *Noor*. Similarly our Prophet's ﷺ nature and reality is *Noor* but he came to this world in human garb as the final Prophet and Guide. His coming into this world in the appearance of a perfect human being is purely by appearance and in no way whatsoever changes his ultimate reality. For example Zaid when in Pakistan wears a Shalwar Kameez but in England wears T-shirt and jeans. His clothes and therefore his appearance changes from place to place but Zaid remains Zaid whether he is in Lahore or London. Without comparison our Prophet ﷺ is *Noor*. By coming to this world as the final Prophet in human garb does not in the slightest change his reality of being made of *Noor*.

# Jibreel ﷺ and the martyrdom news of Imam Hussain

Umme Fazl, wife of Abbas ؓ says that one night she had a dream in which a piece of the Prophet of Allah ﷺ fell into her lap. She was surprised by this dream and went and told the Prophet ﷺ about it. She said: "Ya Rasoolallah! I saw a strange dream in which a piece of you come into my lap." He ﷺ said: "Your dream is a very good one because God willing, Fatima will have a child who will play in your lap." Hence Sayyida Fatima gave birth to Imam Hussain who played in the lap of Umme Fazl.

One day, Imam Hussain was in the lap of the Prophet of Allah ﷺ. Umme Fazl was sitting next to them when she saw tears in his eyes. She asked: "Ya Rasoolallah! Why the tears?" The Prophet ﷺ said: "Sayyiduna Jibreel ﷺ has just come to me and told me that this son of mine will be killed by my Ummah. Jibreel ﷺ has presented to me the soil of the place where he will be killed."

*(Mishkat Sharif, Hujjatullah alal Alameen)*

Sayyiduna Imam Hussain's status and rank is very high. He is the darling of the Prophet of Allah ﷺ. This story shows that the Messenger of Allah ﷺ has been granted knowledge of the unseen because he foretold the birth of Imam Hussain to Fatima. Furthermore he had knowledge of the martyrdom of Imam Hussain and the place where it would take place.

## Response to a question

Some people say that if the Prophet of Allah ﷺ knew that his beloved grandson would be martyred, then why didn't he instruct him not to go there? Why didn't the Messenger of Allah ﷺ say to Imam Hussain "O son! Don't go to Karbala otherwise Yazeed's followers will slaughter you and your family." The answer to this question is that such people that pose such questions are unaware of the high status and rank *Shahadat* has in Islam. Martyrdom in the way of Allah is a very high honour and Allah says the following in the Qur'an about such fortunate people:

**'And don't say that those people who are killed in the way of Allah are dead, nay but they are alive yet you perceive not.'**

*(2:154)*

This verse of the Holy Qur'an clearly states that we cannot call the martyr dead. It may be however that one thinks that Allah has only prohibited us from saying that they are dead but another verse of the Qur'an categorically refutes such notions and states unequivocally the living nature of the martyr:

> **'And those who are killed in Allah's way do not even think they are dead. Indeed they are alive and are with their Lord who is providing for them.'**
>
> *(3:169)*

This is the status of a *Shaheed* in Islam. Allah says that they are alive and after being martyred are being provided for with sustenance by Him. They are alive not dead, yet we do not perceive it.

## But you perceive not

Because we do not perceive their living it does not mean for one moment that they are not alive. Before we were born we were inside our mother's womb for nine months. We were alive during this period of pregnancy but we have no recollection whatsoever of being there. But despite this lack of perception we firmly believe that we were alive for nine months in the womb of our mother before coming into this world. Similarly, if the *Shaheed* is alive in the grave after being killed in the world then why can't we believe that they are alive even though we do not perceive it? We should believe firmly in the verse of the Holy Qur'an that states unequivocally that the *Shaheed* is alive.

## The high status and rank of *Shahadat*

The Prophet of Allah ﷺ said about the eminent rank of *Shahadat*:

**'By Him in Whose Hand my life is, I would love to fight in Allah's Cause and then get martyred and then resurrected (come to life) and then get martyred and then resurrected and then get martyred, and then resurrected and then get martyred and then resurrected.'**

*(Bukhari)*

The Prophet of Allah ﷺ instilled such enthusiasm in his followers for martyrdom that Sayyiduna Umar ﷺ famously supplicated:

**'O Allah! Grant me martyrdom in your cause and let my death be in the city of your Prophet'**

*(Bukhari)*

The pleasure and enjoyment the martyr gets at the time of martyrdom is such that they wish to experience it again and again. The Prophet of Allah ﷺ said:

> 'A person of paradise if given a chance to return to the world would not do so even if they were offered all the wealth of the world. But the *Shaheed* would desire to return to the world and be martyred for the sake of Allah.'
>
> *(Mishkat)*

A poet says:

> **The pleasure the lover (of Allah) expresses for dying**
> **Makes the Messiah and Khidr yearn for it.**

By studying the lives of the Noble Companions, may Allah be pleased with them all, we learn that they were continually in pursuit of martyrdom and its pleasures. The desire was present in the bravest and strongest of men but also in small children. Indeed it was two small boys by the names of Ma'adh and Mu'awwadh who killed the Quraish leader Abu Jahl in the Battle of Badr. This enthusiasm for martyrdom was ever-present not only in the Companions of the Holy Prophet ﷺ but also in his family and this was certainly true in the case of Imam Hasan and Hussain. So why would the Prophet of Allah ﷺ prevent his grandson from attaining the rank of

*Shaheed*, a rank that was destined and written for him on the Preserved Tablet? Furthermore, in response to this question as to why the Prophet of Allah ﷺ did not stop his grandson, we can point out to the following verses and its implications:

> 'Those who deny the signs of Allah
> and slay the prophets unjustly...'
>
> *(3:21)*

And

> '...And that they denied the signs of Allah and slaying
> unjustly the prophets...'
>
> *(4:155)*

These two verses refer to the Jews who killed Allah's prophets without reason. One could argue that if Allah knew that His prophets would be murdered why did He bother sending them? This question — like the original question — posed is a non-starter because it overlooks other facts. The people who pose such questions also state that if the Prophet of Allah ﷺ is a remover of difficulties and aids people at a time of distress then why didn't he help his grandson in Karbala? To this we say that Karbala was the "examination room" in which Imam Hussain was to attain the high status and rank that was to be conferred upon him. The Prophet of Allah ﷺ helped his grandson by instructing him to be patient and perseverant in the face of tyranny and oppression.

## How the Prophet ﷺ helped Imam Hussain at Karbala

To discover how the Prophet of Allah ﷺ helped his grandson in Karbala let us first of all see what Allah says in the Holy Qur'an about help:

> '...And it is on Our binding grace to help the Muslims.'
> *(30:47)*

In other words to help the believers is Allah's responsibility. But how does Allah help?

> 'O Believers! If you help the religion of Allah,
> Allah will help you and will make your feet firm.'
> *(47:7)*

And

> '...And might give courage to your hearts
> and make your steps firm.'
> *(8:11)*

With the help of Allah, believers remain steadfast and fight and die in His path. Historians writing about Karbala say that Imam Hussain ﷺ remained steadfast in his opposition to Yazeed's immorality and corrupt ways. From Madinah to Karbala the Prophet of Allah ﷺ would appear in his darling grandson's dream and instruct him with patience and steadfastness in the face of adversity. It was with the help of the supplications of the Prophet of Allah ﷺ that Imam Hussain and his followers remained steadfast in this ordeal and passed the examination they were sitting and tasted the divine cup of *Shahadat* and all its pleasures. His resolute stance and impeccable behaviour from Madinah to Makkah and then on his journey to Karbala will remain a prime example of resoluteness. Indeed Imam Hussain is *Sayyidus Shuhada* - the leader of Martyrs.

## The Prophet's ﷺ tears

When the Prophet of Allah ﷺ heard the news of his darling grandson's martyrdom from Jibreel ﷺ, tears emerged from his beautiful eyes. We learn that it is natural to shed tears on hearing the news of martyrdom and hence it is permissible to do so. The limitation of grief however is crying and no further. To weep bitterly out of control and to slap the chest is not permitted. In the Holy Qur'an we find reference to

Sayyiduna Ayub ﷺ who cried so much at the loss of his beloved son Yusuf ﷺ that his eyes turned white in sorrow. The words of the Qur'an are '...and his eyes were whitened with grief...' (12:84). The commentators of Qur'an say that his eyes turned white and his vision became extremely weak. His pain of separation was true and so were his tears. So we ask the question that today if people weep out of control in the pain of the martyrdom of Imam Hussain then surely their eyes should turn white and have poor vision? The fact of the matter is that their claim to love Imam Hussain and the Ahle Bayt is false and so are their tears.

## Contempt of Ahle Bayt

So far we have seen what great honour and rank martyrdom has in Islam and heard what the Messenger of Allah ﷺ has said about it. But now let us see how some claimants of loving the Ahle Bayt in actual fact dishonour and insult them, this narration is from *Usul Kaafi*, a leading Shia book.

"Imam Jafar narrates that Jibreel ﷺ came to the Prophet of Allah ﷺ and gave him the *Basharat* (good news) that Fatima would have a child but who would be martyred by his Ummah. The Prophet of Allah ﷺ said: "I have no need for Fatima's child if he is to be murdered by followers." Jibreel ﷺ returned to the heavens and then went to the Prophet ﷺ again and gave the same news. The Prophet ﷺ again said that he had no desire for such a child. Jibreel ﷺ then went to the heavens again and returned this time with the news for the Prophet ﷺ that Allah ﷻ will make the progeny of this child one of *Imamat* and *Wilayat*. The Prophet ﷺ heard this and accepted the child. The Prophet ﷺ then went to Fatima to give news of her new child. He told her that his followers would murder her child. Fatima said that she had no desire for such a child that was murdered by his followers. The Prophet ﷺ sent another message to her telling her that the child will be father to spiritual leaders and saints. Fatima heard this and accepted the child."

It is self evident that this insulting and contemptuous narration from *Usul Kaafi*, a "leading" book of the Shias, shows that (Allah forbid) the Prophet of Allah ﷺ and Sayyida Fatima were ungrateful and unaware of the status of *Shahadat* and that their constant refusal of Jibreel's ﷺ message was clear contempt of Allah's will. We conclude from such a fabrication that such people are not only in contempt of the Noble Companions but also of the Ahle Bayt, the people they claim to ardently love. May Allah protect us from such heretical beliefs- Ameen.

# Jibreel's علیہ السلام observation

Once the Prophet of Allah ﷺ asked Jibreel علیہ السلام whether he saw a being like him in the East or West? Jibreel علیہ السلام replied: "O Prophet! I have seen the East and the West and I have not seen a being better or like you. Ya Rasoolallah! Your Lord says that if I made Ibrahim علیہ السلام my *Khaleel* then I have made you my *Habib* and that He has not created anyone more beloved than you and that He has made the world and its inhabitants for the sole purpose of knowing your high rank and My closeness to you which is my *Izzat* (honour). Allah says: "O Beloved! If I did not make you I would not have made the world."

*(Hujjatullah Alal Alameen)*

Jibreel's علیہ السلام opinion and observation was that there was no one better in the East or West than the Beloved of Allah ﷺ. Furthermore, Allah added His comments when he told the Prophet ﷺ through Jibreel علیہ السلام about his high status and rank. The *Khaleel* seeks the happiness (*Rida*) of Allah but Allah seeks the happiness of the *Habib*. Prophets Adam's selection,

Moses's speech and Jesus's prayer, the Prophet Muhammad ﷺ is the collection of all these things. Moreover he has the quality of being Allah's Beloved, a status no other Prophet has been granted.

## Molvi Ismail's observation

Allah Almighty has created the entire universe for the status and honour of His Beloved but Molvi Ismail Dehlvi writes "Everything whether it is a Prophet or not in the sight of Allah is the same and as disgraceful as a cobbler." *(Taqwiyatul Iman)* This contemptuous and despicable statement is in direct contradiction to the will of Allah. The reality of creation is clearly illustrated in the narration cited above. Allah says that he would not have created anything had it not been for His Beloved ﷺ. Molvi Ismail Dehlvi for some inexplicable reason thinks otherwise. Who should we believe?

Imam Ahmad Raza Khan expresses the reality in the following beautiful way

*Zammino Zamaan tumhare liye*
*Makino Makan tumhare liye*
*Chunino Chuna tumhare liye*
*Bane do jahan tumhare liye.*

The earth and the time are made for your sake
The dwellers and their abodes are made for you
The 'why' and 'how' (knowledge) is there for you
The two worlds were created for you.

# Jibreel's عليه السلام request

On the night of Isra and Miraj, Jibreel عليه السلام accompanied the Prophet of Allah ﷺ but when they reached the *Sidra* - the Lote Tree - he told his Master that he could travel no further. The Prophet of Allah ﷺ asked him why. He replied that his wings would melt and perish due to the intensity of light beyond *Sidra*. Jibreel عليه السلام said to the Prophet ﷺ that only he could go beyond this point. The Prophet of Allah ﷺ asked Jibreel عليه السلام if he had any request that he could present to Allah Almighty to be accepted on this auspicious occasion. Jibreel عليه السلام replied that he had one request and that was that on the Day of Judgement when his believers would be crossing the bridge over hell to reach paradise, it was his wish that he could lay his wings on the bridge so that the faithful could cross safely into paradise.

*(Al-Mawahib al-Laduniyya)*

Sayyiduna Jibreel ﷺ is the leader of the angels. On the night of Miraj at the place of *Sidra* he told his Master that he could go no further and that to go beyond *Sidra* was beyond his station. Jibreel ﷺ here submitted and acknowledged that the status of the Prophet ﷺ is greatest in creation and beyond the realm of *Sidra* that even the leader of angels cannot go. We learn then that Jibreel ﷺ acknowledged that he was not like the Beloved Prophet ﷺ because for Jibreel ﷺ to go past *Sidra* would have meant annihilation but for the Prophet of Allah ﷺ it would symbolise even further his high status and rank. The Messenger of Allah ﷺ is without likeness and Jibreel ﷺ knew this, because firstly, he did not attempt to go beyond *Sidra* himself and secondly, he did not try and stop the Beloved of Allah ﷺ from going further. The angels know this and acknowledge that they are not like him and he is not like them, but some so called Muslims believe he is just like them. So who are we to believe and follow?

## *Waseela* (means)

The Prophet of Allah ﷺ said to Jibreel ﷺ that if he had any request or wish he should inform him so he could present it to Allah Almighty for it to be accepted. Hence the Prophet of Allah ﷺ from this act was making apparent that the real fulfiller of needs is Allah Almighty but being made through his *Waseela* enhances its effectiveness. If the *Waseela* of the Prophet ﷺ were not needed then Jibreel علیہ السلام would have said to the Prophet ﷺ that if he had any request he would have done it directly, but Jibreel علیہ السلام did not say that or think like that because he appreciated the real status and lofty station of the Holy Prophet ﷺ. What Jibreel علیہ السلام did was to request to the Prophet ﷺ to allow him to come to the aid of his Ummah and lay his wings below the bridge so that the believers can cross safely. Imam Ahmad Raza Khan expresses his feelings about crossing the bridge on the Day of Judgement in the following way:

> **Help me cross the bridge,**
> **so that the bridge does not know I have passed,**
> **And when Jibreel spreads his wings, let me cross**
> **so that the wings do not know I have passed!**

We learn from this story that Jibreel علیہ السلام, the courtier of the Prophet's ﷺ court, has love and affection for the Ummah that he wished to help us in our hour of need.

# Jibreel ﷺ and the angel of death

The Prophet of Allah ﷺ fell ill. Jibreel ﷺ appeared before the Prophet of Allah ﷺ and said: "Ya Rasoolallah! Allah gives you His greetings and asks how you are, although He knows your condition better than you, yet He desires to increase your dignity and honour." The Prophet of Allah ﷺ replied that he was in pain. The next day, Jibreel ﷺ appeared before the Prophet ﷺ and asked him how he was. The Prophet of Allah ﷺ gave the same answer. Jibreel ﷺ appeared on the third day and said: "O Prophet! With me today is an angel named Ismail who is here to enquire about your health." The Prophet ﷺ asked who he was. "Angel Ismail is the leader of one hundred thousand angels and each of these angels are leaders of one hundred thousand angels." Jibreel ﷺ also informed him that the angel of death was present and was seeking his permission to do his duty. "This is unprecedented that he seeks permission and never again will he seek permission from the person in removing their soul. If you give permission O Prophet! Then he can come and do his duty." The Prophet ﷺ gave permission. Hence the angel of death presented himself to the Prophet ﷺ and said: "O Prophet! Truly Allah yearns to see you. He has sent me to do my duty and He has ordered me to seek your permission to do it, but if you so wish then I will return because Allah has told me to do whatever you command." The Prophet of Allah ﷺ said: "Will you do as I say?" The angel of death said "Yes." The Prophet ﷺ looked towards Jibreel ؈ who said to the Prophet ﷺ: "O Muhammad ﷺ! Your Lord is waiting for you!" The Prophet ﷺ said to the angel of death that he had his permission to take his soul. Jibreel ؈ said: "Peace be upon you O Prophet of Allah! This is the final time I shall descend to the earth (to serve you) as I have no purpose save being present with you." The angel of death then took the soul of the Prophet of Allah ﷺ out of his blessed and pure body.

*(Mishkat Sharif, Al-Mawahib al-Laduniyya)*

The Prophet's ﷺ status is such that the Almighty who has no need for anything or anyone is asking about his wellbeing even though He is all-Knowing and all-Seeing. It is a sign of friendship to ask a friend how they are. The Prophet of Allah ﷺ is no ordinary being and this is no ordinary friendship! We are talking here about Allah and His *Habib* (beloved). How could it possibly be that the Loved does not ask the Beloved about his well-being? But Allah is Lord and is free from time and space and hence sent Jibreel ؈ as a messenger to ask how he was. We learn from this that it is not necessary that the questioner be without knowledge of the issue. Asking something despite having full knowledge of it is sometimes an act of wisdom and this is one such example. In taking the soul of the Prophet ﷺ the angel of death did not go alone. With him was Jibreel ؑ and Ismail, an angel who was chief of one hundred thousand angels who themselves were leaders of one hundred thousand angels. The angel of death sought permission from the Prophet ﷺ, something that he had never done before and with the exception of the Prophet ﷺ, will never do again. The Prophet of Allah ﷺ was given the choice of when he wanted to die and leave this world. Our reality is that we had no choice in the matter as to when we came into the world and we certainly do not have a say in the matter when we leave this world. So how can some people claim that they are like the Prophet ﷺ? Did these people have a say in their entry into the world and will they call the angel of death when it suits them? Certainly not! How foolish are such ignorant people who fail to realise the reality of the Prophet of Allah ﷺ. Have they not read the incident of Prophet Musa ؑ and the angel of death?!

# Jibreel's علیہ السلام glad tidings

Sayyiduna Jibreel علیہ السلام came to the Prophet of Allah ﷺ near to the time of his death and said: "Ya Rasoolallah! Today the heavens are being prepared for your reception. Allah has told Malik, the doorkeeper of Hell, to extinguish the fire of Hell as today your soul will travel through the heavens. Allah has ordered the heavenly maidens (Houri) to decorate the heavens and all the angels have been ordered to stand in rows in anticipation of your soul's passage from your body to the Almighty. I have been ordered to come to you with the glad tidings that He shall not disappoint you regarding your Ummah. Their reckoning will be swiftest on the Day of Judgement, and that Paradise is forbidden for all the other Prophets and nations until your Ummah has entered Paradise. I am also told to inform you O Prophet of Allah ﷺ that on the Day of Judgement Allah will forgive your Ummah so that you will be satisfied."

*(Madaarij al-Nabuwwa)*

On receiving the soul of the Holy Prophet ﷺ, Allah ordered that the Paradise be decorated and that all preparations were made for a magnificent reception befitting for the Beloved of Allah. The angels and Houri were rejoicing at the coming of the Prophet ﷺ to them. When the Prophet ﷺ left this mortal world the creatures of the hereafter rejoiced in such a befitting manner and for this reason the true believers in this world rejoice in remembering the coming of the Holy Prophet ﷺ to this world, namely the *Mawlid un Nabi* by decorating and illuminating their homes and streets. Respect and honour of the Holy Prophet ﷺ is the will of Allah and it is the way of the angels and Houri. Not only was the Paradise decorated but also the Hell fire was extinguished. There are people whose fire of anger burn at the sight of people revering and honouring the Prophet of Allah ﷺ particularly at the time of *Mawlid un Nabi*. Most poignantly, Allah's Messenger at this moment in time showed concern for his followers and Allah allayed his fears with a truly wonderful piece of news for us sinful believers.

Khuda ki raza chahata hein do alam
Khuda chahata hein raza e Muhammad ﷺ

The creation wishes the happiness of its Lord
The Lord wishes the happiness of Muhammad ﷺ